Essential Histories

The French
Revolutionary Wars

Essential Histories

The French
Revolutionary Wars

Gregory Fremont-Barnes

First published in Great Britain in 2001 by Osprey Publishing,
Midland House, West Way, Botley, Oxford OX2 0PH, UK
44-02 23rd St, Suite 219, Long Island City, NY 11101, USA
Email: info@ospreypublishing.com

Every attempt has been made by the publisher to secure the appropriate permissions for
material reproduced in this book. If there has been any oversight we will be happy to rectify
the situation and written submission should be made to the Publishers.

Transferred to digital print on demand 2010

First published 2001
2nd impression 2008

Printed and bound by PrintOnDemand-Worldwide.com, Peterborough, UK

A CIP catalogue record for this book is available from the British Library

ISBN: 978 1 84176 283 8

Editorial by Rebecca Cullen
Design by Ken Vail Graphic Design, Cambridge, UK
Cartography by The Map Studio
Index by Susan Williams
Picture research by Image Select International
Originated by PPS Grasmere Ltd., Leeds, UK
Typeset in Monotype Gill Sans and ITC Stone Serif

The Woodland Trust
Osprey Publishing is supporting the Woodland Trust, the UK's leading woodland conservation charity,
by funding the dedication of trees.

www.ospreypublishing.com

Contents

Major actions on land 1792–1800

Europe as it appeared at the start of the French Revolutionary Wars

1. **France** Valmy (1792), Valenciennes, Perpignan, Truillas, Hondschoote, and Wattignies (1793), Le Boulon and Tourcoing (1794).

2. **Belgium** Jemappes (1792), Neerwinden, (1793), Courtrai, Tournai and Fleurus (1794).

3. **Holland** Bergen, twice, and Castricum (1799).

4. **Germany** Amberg, Friedberg, Wurzburg, Schliengen (1796), Stockach (1799), Hochstadt and Hohenlinden (1800).

5. **Switzerland** Zurich – three times (1799).

6. **Italy** Loano (1795), Montenotte, Dego, Mondovi, Lodi, Lonato, Castiglione, Bassano, Caldiero and Arcola (1796), Rivoli (1797), Magnano, Cassano, The Trebbia and Novi (1799), Montebello and Marengo (1800).

7. **Spain** Campródon, San Marcial and Figueras (1794).

8. **The Middle East** The Pyramids (1798), Mount Tabor and Aboukir (1799), Heliopolis (1800) and Alexandria, twice (1801). Important sieges: Lille, Longwy and Verdun (1792); Valenciennes, Condé, Mainz, Quesnoy, Dunkirk and Toulon (1793); Collioure (1794), Rosas, Luxembourg (1795), Mantua (1796–97); Valetta (1798–1800); Acre and Milan (1799); Genoa (1800).

Introduction

Two centuries now separate us from the series of conflicts known as the French Revolutionary Wars. These wars, fought by armies of unprecedented size, in the course of a single decade (1792–1802) thrust upon an unwilling continent political, social, and military changes of such radical proportions that they forever changed the Western world. For the first time in European history war unleashed ideological forces whose power and appeal called into question the principle that underpinned the European political system: the principle of monarchy. The French Revolutionaries, in challenging the political legitimacy of the *ancien régime*, laid the foundations for the widespread acceptance of democratic, representative, and constitutional rule. Wherever their armies went they brought with them the abstract notions of 'Nation' and 'People'. Here began a new phase in the history of warfare whose impact is still seen today in the existence of mass citizen-armies. The precedent was set, through universal conscription and the systematic marshaling of national resources, for 'total' war.

The greatest naval and military figures of modern times – Nelson and Napoleon – came to the fore during this period. They were to reach their respective heights only a short time later in the Napoleonic Wars (1803–15). Indeed, the French Revolutionary Wars were fought in an age when leaders and men still regarded war as 'glorious' and the cult of the hero was at its pitch. The Revolutionary Wars were the first proving-ground for the band of charismatic and colorful men who were to serve as marshals under the French Empire. Most of Napoleon's great marshals and Nelson's able lieutenants gained their experience at this time. Augereau, Jourdan, Masséna, Kellermann and many others proved themselves on the fields of Belgium and Germany, the plains of northern Italy and on the sands of Egypt and Syria.

The Revolutionary Wars were fought on a vast geographical scale. They raged across much of western and central Europe, the Middle East, southern Africa and the West Indies. At sea, rival navies struggled for supremacy in all the waters around Europe, the Atlantic, the Caribbean, the Indian Ocean and beyond. When we consider their extent it should perhaps not surprise us that contemporaries and 19th-century historians referred to these conflicts, in conjunction with the Napoleonic Wars, as 'the Great War'.

The French Revolutionary Wars were more than just the last conflict of a century already riven by intense strife; they marked an abrupt and shattering end to the era of 'limited' wars which had begun in the age of Enlightenment. Up until this time, rival dynasties ruling absolutely over their feudal societies matched the power of their small, meticulously trained, highly expensive professional forces in the quest for territorial spoil or economic advantage without radically upsetting the existing balance of power between great empires.

The wars of the French Revolution swept all that into the dustbin of history. Here was a new and epic struggle, which the revolutionaries characterized as a life or death contest between the forces of liberty, equality, and fraternity, on the one hand, and the corrupt despotism of the *ancien régimes* on the other. Indeed, for France the early years were nothing less than a fight for political survival, with cries of *'la Patrie en danger!'* coming from all quarters. Yet even before security from invasion was assured the war aims of the Revolutionaries took a radical turn: the 'liberation' of their oppressed brethren in the Low Countries and the Rhineland became the new objective. And, finally, emboldened by victories, the noble aims of the Revolution had been forgotten and the whole movement appeared to have lost its early idealism. What had begun as an ideological struggle, within a few, turbulent years developed into a simple war of territorial expansion in the great traditions of the revolutionaries' monarchist political forebears. It was a supreme irony indeed, and by 1795 – for the first time since the Carolingian kings of the 9th century – France stood triumphant on her 'natural' frontiers: the Rhine, the Alps, and the Pyrenees. She achieved what both Louis XIV and Louis XV had failed to do earlier in the century despite the kings' enormous expenditure in men and money.

The Revolutionary Wars mark the beginning of modern war not because of the introduction of new technology, but because they established the idea of the great citizen-army now so familiar to us today. Universal conscription implemented with organizational genius by Lazare Carnot enabled France to field vast new armies. These, composed of men fired with patriotic enthusiasm, were used not only to hold back the tide of counter-revolution, but to cross the French frontiers taking with them the seeds of republicanism. Marching to the strains of the Marseillaise and with cries of 'Vive la Republic!', these 'armed missionaries', as Robespierre termed them, introduced forms of political and social changes which opponents of the Revolution could not contain.

The wars revolutionized warfare itself, with the use of light troops, the deployment of armies by corps and divisions, the use of concentration both tactically and strategically to bring maximum force to bear on a weaker opponent, and, above all, the principle of 'living off the land' rather than depending exclusively on depots and enormous supply trains. Gone forever were the days when civilians lived a separate existence from the conflicts waged by their respective sovereigns. For occupied peoples,

the French Revolutionary Wars brought conflict directly to the home front through the permanent presence of foreign armies, conscription, wholesale requisitioning and heavy, sometimes crippling, taxation. In France, particularly, war made hitherto unheard of demands on its citizens, thus establishing the close link between soldier and civilian so familiar to the generations which fought the World Wars more than a century later.

The wars placed into the hands of the Revolutionary government in France power which the European monarchs could not have imagined – power which translated itself into armies whose combination of sheer size and patriotic fervor drove them across Europe, defying all who stood in their paths. Indeed, so great was the military power unleashed by the Revolution that nothing less than the whole of Europe, seven coalitions and a generation of fighting were required finally to bring France to heel.

Politically, the Revolutionary Wars opened a Pandora's box which even the final allied victory in 1815 could not completely close. As the revolutionary armies marched triumphant across the Low Countries, Germany, Italy, and Switzerland they laid the groundwork of nationalism and constitutional rule so necessary for a strong sense of nationhood or, in some cases, future unification. The wars brought an effective end to the Holy Roman Empire. Prussia's status and influence within Germany were therefore increased. This had far-reaching implications. Prussia ultimately became a far more aggressive state than Austria ever was and would become a menace to European security after German unification in 1871. By eliminating dozens of antiquated princedoms and electorates, France inadvertently opened the way for eventual German unification under Prussian leadership.

The French Revolutionary Wars included some of history's most dramatic battles on land as well as at sea – and no previous conflict boasted so many. Seldom have wars *begun* with battles so decisive not only for the immediate conflict itself, but for history in general. Valmy did just that. A few hours' cannonade brought a halt to the carefully dressed ranks of Prussian infantry, that great legacy of Frederick the Great. This exchange itself illustrates the emergence of the new citizen-soldier and the decline of the 'walking muskets' of absolutism. As Marshal Foch declared a century later, 'The wars of kings were at an end. The wars of peoples were beginning.' Lodi, though not in itself more than a minor engagement, nevertheless symbolized the spirit of the age, with the young, energetic Bonaparte, flag in hand, leading his men across a heavily defended bridge, driving before him a vastly superior force.

Battles at sea were no less significant. At Cape St Vincent, off the Spanish coast, Horatio Nelson's success bore out his policy of ignoring orthodox naval tactics. The following year, with his crushing victory at the Nile, Nelson would end forever Bonaparte's dream of establishing an Eastern empire and threatening British rule in India. And there was Marengo – where after driving his weary men over the Alps in the great traditions of Hannibal, Bonaparte snatched victory from the jaws of defeat, leaving Austria defenseless in Italy and almost incapable of further resistance.

Although France ultimately attained supremacy on land, Britain had swept the oceans of the French merchant marine, snapped up most of France's colonies, and had consistently defeated her navy in great fleet actions which so reduced French power at sea as to render the outcome at Trafalgar almost a foregone conclusion. Naval power complemented and sustained Britain's commercial and financial strength. Britain was able to establish and maintain two great coalitions, only to see them crushed by her seemingly invincible counterpart on land. After a decade of conflict France had vanquished all the Continent's great powers – Austria, Prussia, and Russia – leaving an uneasy and temporary stalemate with Britain mistress of the seas and France master on land.

In 1802, Napoleon inherited a French Republic greatly enlarged and supremely self-confident. He was by then not simply a leader of men but a leader of the nation. His unrivalled success in the Revolutionary Wars gave him the authority he needed to seize political power in France, and also a mandate to prosecute war on an even greater scale than before, so building – and ultimately losing – the greatest empire in Europe since Rome.

Chronology

1789 14 July Storming of the Bastille. A Paris mob seizes the infamous state prison and fortress, signaling the revolt against the monarchy and established authority.

1791 2 August Declaration of Pillnitz. Prussia and Austria declare their intention to form a general European coalition to restore the Bourbon monarchy in France.

1792 7 February Conclusion of Austro-Prussian Alliance. Troops begin advance toward French frontier; Sardinia (Piedmont) joins soon after.

20 April French declare war on Austria. Hostilities begin in Flanders.

20 September Battle of Valmy. Dumouriez and Kellermann, with 59,000 men, confront and drive away 35,000 Prussians by cannon fire alone. The Allied advance on Paris is temporarily checked; the Revolution is saved.

6 November Battle of Jemappes. Austrian defeat leads to the fall of Brussels to the French, who then lay siege to Antwerp, causing alarm in Britain.

1793 21 January Execution of Louis XVI, outraging the crowned heads of Europe; national conscription called; Belgium annexed; invasion of Holland imminent.

1 February France declares war on Britain and Holland, then against Spain (March 7).

18 March Battle of Neerwinden. Austrians repulse French under Dumouriez.

23 August *Levée en masse*. French government decrees universal male conscription.

27 August–19 December Siege of Toulon. Royalist forces, backed by an Anglo-Spanish fleet and troops, fail to hold the city.

8 September Battle of Hondschoote. Houchard with 24,000 French defeats 16,000 men under the Duke of York.

1794 23 May Battle of Tournai. Drawn action between equal forces; both sides retreat.

1 June Battle of the Glorious First of June. British naval victory; Howe defeats his rival but fails to prevent a vital food convoy from reaching France.

26 June Battle of Fleurus. Kléber defeats Saxe-Coburg's attempts to relieve Charleroi.

1795 January–March French Occupation of both Belgium and Holland.

5 April–22 June Treaty of Basle. Prussia, plus several minor German states, leaves the war. Spain follows suit.

1796 27 March Bonaparte assumes command of the Army of Italy.

10 May Battle of Lodi. Bonaparte personally leads the attack over the bridge and secures victory. Milan is captured (May 15) and peace reached with Piedmont. France annexes Nice and Savoy.

5 August Battle of Castiglione. Bonaparte turns both flanks of Würmser's army, forcing it across the Mincio River.

19 August Treaty of San Ildefonso. Spain becomes a French ally, threatening the Royal Navy's presence in the Mediterranean.

3 September Battle of Würzburg. Archduke Charles of Austria defeats Jourdan.

8 September Battle of Bassano. French defeat the Austrians, who retreat into the besieged city of Mantua.

15–17 November Battle of Arcola. Bonaparte, with the able assistance of Augereau and Masséna, defeats the Austrians.

1797 **14 January** Battle of Rivoli. Significant French victory over the Austrians.

14 February Battle of Cape St Vincent. Admiral Jervis defeats a Spanish fleet with a vital contribution from Nelson.

17 October Treaty of Campo Formio. Austria recognizes French annexation of Belgium; France establishes satellite Cisalpine Republic in northern Italy; Austria compensated with Republic of Venice; most of the left bank of the Rhine becomes French.

1798 **19 May** Expedition to Egypt begins. Bonaparte embarks from Toulon with the Army of the Orient.

21 July Battle of the Pyramids. Bonaparte repulses Mameluke forces near Gizeh.

July–August Occupation of Egypt.

1 August Battle of the Nile. Nelson decisively defeats Bruey's fleet in Aboukir Bay, leaving Bonaparte's army stranded in Egypt.

24 December Anglo-Russian alliance establishes the basis for the Second Coalition, which includes Austria, Portugal, Naples, and Turkey.

1799 **March** Jourdan invades Germany; operations begin in Switzerland.

25 March Battle of Stockach. Jourdan retreats to the Rhine after serious defeat at the hands of Archduke Charles.

5 April Battle of Magnano. Austrians defeat the French under Schérer.

17 April Battle of Mount Tabor. Bonaparte drives off a Turkish force during his campaign in Syria.

27 April Battle of Cassano. Moreau defeated. Russian troops under Suvorov enter Milan (April 28) and soon after Turin.

5 June Masséna repulses the Austrians at Zürich but is forced to withdraw by overwhelming numbers.

17–19 June Battle of the Trebbia. Suvorov defeats Macdonald and pushes the French back to the Riviera

August–October Anglo-Russian operations in the Netherlands. The Allies' campaign is withdrawn as a failure. The Dutch fleet is, however, captured in the Texel.

15 August Battle of Novi. The Russians decisively defeat the French, allowing Suvorov to pursue them across the Apennines.

25 September Third Battle of Zürich. Masséna severely defeats the Russians, bringing the campaign to an end.

4 November Battle of Genoa. Austrian victory; French retreat back over the Alps.

1800 **8 March** Bonaparte raises a new army. Having returned from Egypt, he plans to invade northern Italy and reverse French misfortunes.

14 June Battle of Marengo. Significant Austrian defeat, Bonaparte's greatest victory thus far.

3 December Battle of Hohenlinden. Brilliant French victory over Archduke John in southern Germany.

1801 **9 February** Treaty of Lunéville. Austria withdraws from the Second Coalition; terms of Campo Formio reconfirmed.

March–August British operations in Egypt. The French capitulate on 31 August and are shipped back home.

2 April Battle of Copenhagen. Nelson crushes the Danish fleet, effectively ending the League of Armed Neutrality.

1802 **27 March** Treaty of Amiens. Establishment of peace between Britain and France, ending the French Revolutionary Wars.

Historical rivalries

On the eve of the French Revolution the political construction of Europe was remarkably simple. The Continent was dominated by five great powers: Britain, France, Austria, Russia, and Prussia. Their weaker neighbors – Sweden, Spain, Poland, Holland, and Turkey – had all once enjoyed periods of economic, military, or naval greatness, but by the end of the 18th century had slipped into the ranks of the lesser powers. Most of western Germany remained fragmented into hundreds of minor principalities, ecclesiastical cities, and minor states contained within the Holy Roman Empire. Italy, similarly, contained a number of small kingdoms, some independent and others controlled by Austria.

Europe was overwhelmingly agrarian and feudal, particularly in the east, with monarchs ruling absolutely within their domains. Britain was a somewhat different case: though the vast majority of her people were disenfranchised, the monarchy ruled under constitutional constraints. The nation's prosperity was based not on agriculture but on trade. The process of industrialization, though still in its infancy, was well under way.

A generation before the French Revolution, Prussia, under the ruling house of Hohenzollern, had established herself as Europe's newest great power, having won a series of costly and exhausting wars in which she had taken on and defeated practically every major state on the Continent. Frederick the Great had inherited from his father, Frederick William (1713–40), a highly militarized, extremely efficient state where the landed aristocracy and king enjoyed a close relationship. The aristocracy were freeholders of their land and, in effect, over their peasants as well. In return, the crown taxed the nation heavily in order to maintain a standing army proportionally much larger than that of any other European state. Frederick used that army aggressively: he invaded Austrian Silesia in 1740, and thus began the War of the Austrian Succession (1740–48). This was followed by the Seven Years' War (1756–63) (see Osprey Essential HIstories, *The Seven Years' War*, by Daniel Marston) in which Prussia used her formidable army for the glory of the nation and to consolidate her territorial gains, generally at the expense of Austria. During the Seven Years' War Frederick fought the greatest coalition ever seen in Europe – Austria, France, Russia, Sweden, and most of the German states of the Holy Roman Empire – and survived intact. It was the hard-fought bloody encounters of this war that confirmed for Prussia her place among the Great Powers.

The Russian Empire covered a vast stretch of territory containing at the turn of the century about 48 million subjects, over half of whom were serfs tied to the land. The autocratic Romanov dynasty had ruled since the early 17th century. Russia's military reputation had been won under Peter the Great, who had defeated the Swedes in the Great Northern War (1700–21). Although Russia had briefly fought Prussia in the later years of the Seven Years' War, her territorial gains were made at Polish and Turkish expense during the reign of Catherine the Great (1762–96), particularly during the First Partition of Poland in 1772 and in the annexation of the Crimea, an Ottoman possession, in 1783.

Russia fought simultaneous conflicts with Sweden (1788–90) and, in alliance with Austria, Turkey (1787–92). She was ultimately successful in both of these conflicts. When the French Revolutionary Wars began, Catherine the Great remained neutral and she died four years later in 1796 without having challenged the Revolution. That task was left to her son and successor, Paul I, who would finally face France during the War of the Second Coalition (1798–1802). Paul was known for his mental instability and obsession with military matters and was assassinated in 1801.

George III, who had presided over the somewhat different and more constitutional monarchy of Britain since 1760, proved to be one of the Revolution's most implacable opponents. Political power rested with Parliament and the Prime Minister. William Pitt the Younger had attained office in 1783 with a loyal following in the House of Commons and the support of the crown. Though small by continental standards – with a population of fewer than 10 million – Britain was the world's most prosperous nation. Her wealth was based on thriving trade with Europe and her exclusive access to a vast empire which, in addition to Canada and, above all, India, included newly acquired territories in Australia and many of the bountiful 'sugar islands' of the West Indies. As international trade was the basis of the rapidly increasing national wealth, the protection of trade was paramount. Britain's unrivalled merchant fleet, which exceeded 10,000 vessels, could confidently rely on the power of the Royal Navy for its protection. Although agriculture was still important – accounting for one-third of the national product – Britain was the birthplace of the recent phenomenon of industrialization, and its growing manufacturing capacity played a major role in stimulating a booming economy.

Britain and France were long-standing enemies, having fought one another regularly over the past century and on opposite sides in nearly every conflict in which the two countries were engaged since the Middle Ages. Indeed, the French Revolutionary Wars were just the latest conflict in a long succession dating back to Louis XIV which historians would later refer to as the second Hundred Years' War. The roots of Anglo-French hostility were political and economic. Britain was chiefly concerned with preventing the French from dominating the

George III. By the time Britain entered the Revolutionary Wars he had already reigned for 33 years, during which time he had presided over the loss of the American colonies. He suffered from periodic fits of madness, but his eccentricities did not adversely affect his conduct as sovereign during the 1790s. Indeed, his own patriotic idealism enhanced his popular reputation. He opposed the Revolution on ideological grounds and sharply condemned the execution of his brother sovereign, Louis XVI. (Ann Ronan Picture Library)

Continent. The cornerstone of this policy was the protection of the Low Countries and the Channel ports, in support of which aim Britain had participated in the Wars of the Spanish and Austrian Successions, challenging France in Europe as well as overseas. The two powers were traditional colonial and commercial rivals. Britain had fought over North America and India, and at the end of the Seven Years' War Britain was in possession of the whole of Canada and the American colonies, together with large portions of the subcontinent. France had exacted a degree of revenge by providing vital

Emperor Francis II of Austria. Succeeding to the throne in 1792 just as relations with France were worsening, his opposition to the Revolution helped bring the two nations closer to war. Francis accompanied his troops during part of the campaign in Flanders during 1793–94. Throughout the wars his policies shifted under the influence of court and military factions which divided his counsels between doves and hawks. (Roger-Viollet)

aid to the American colonies during the War of Independence (1775–83), a war that deprived Britain of an important piece of her empire and left her in serious debt.

At the start of the French Revolution Austria was ruled by Joseph II, brother to Marie Antoinette. As head of the Habsburg monarchy he also held the title of Holy Roman Emperor, which enabled him to exercise considerable political influence over a large number of small German states, many bordering France, whose existence stretched back to the days of Charlemagne. Francis II (1768–1835) succeeded to the throne in 1792. He held personal control of affairs through a council of ministers, although regional diets, or parliaments, administered Hungary, Holland, and lands in Italy. His domains were vast and stretched from northern Italy, across Austria proper,

Hungary, parts of Poland and portions of the Balkans, to the Netherlands (roughly modern Belgium). The number of nationalities – the empire included Germans, Hungarians, Czechs, Italians, Poles, Croats, and others, totaling about 27 million subjects in 1800, with 250,000 in Vienna – and geographical circumstances (the fact that, for example, Belgium was not contiguous to Austria) rendered the empire less cohesive than the states of western Europe.

Austria had been repeatedly defeated: by France during the War of the Polish Succession (1733–35); by the Turks during a Balkan war from 1737 to 1739, and, as already noted, by Prussia in a series of major conflicts between 1740 and 1763, during the reign of Maria Theresa. Not only did the Empress suffer loss of territory, she jealously witnessed the slowly rising influence of Prussia in German affairs. Her successor had his own share of problems. In 1787, Joseph II had been obliged to go to war against Turkey after the Turks declared war on Austria's ally, Russia. As the Russians soon became enmeshed in a simultaneous war with the Swedes in the north, this left Joseph alone to take on the Turks in the south, where they briefly invaded southern Hungary. To complicate matters, the Austrian possessions in the Low Countries rose in revolt in 1789. Yet in the meantime the Turks were defeated, Belgrade taken and the war ended in the same year. The Habsburg monarchy thus continued to enjoy its status as a great power when war again loomed after the revolution in France.

France possessed an illustrious military past, though the wars of the 18th century had done much to erode this reputation. Since the 16th century her rivalry with Habsburg Spain and Austria had formed the pillars of her foreign policy, and the conflicts that resulted enabled France to expand her territory and commerce to such a degree that under Louis XIV she was Europe's foremost military power. Louis continued to challenge Habsburg power, particularly in the Low Countries and regularly fought Britain both in Europe and overseas. Yet the War of the

Spanish Succession did not yield the Low Countries, as France had hoped, and in later years, in spite of several successful campaigns during the War of the Austrian Succession, France was obliged to return to Austria the conquests in the Netherlands she had made during that conflict. During the 'diplomatic revolution' of 1756 she made amends with her long-time Habsburg foe and allied herself with Austria to take on Prussia, as well as her great colonial and commercial rival, Britain.

However, France suffered catastrophically as a result of the Seven Years' War, losing Canada to Britain, and also many of her possessions in the West Indies and most of those in India. Thus France was in decline, and although she was instrumental in ensuring the success of the rebel cause during the War of American Independence, the Treaty of Paris offered independence to the Americans and territorial gain to Spain but virtually nothing to France. The halcyon days of Louis XIV were now long in the past. France's wars had not only cost her dear in colonies and men, but they were also crippling financially. The strain on the French economy and the threat of bankruptcy obliged ministers to institute radical reforms, beginning in 1787, which required the imposition of new taxes. In order to pass these reforms, Louis XVI required the

The Storming of the Bastille, 14 July 1789. The great state prison in Paris held only seven inmates but a large quantity of weapons and gunpowder eagerly sought by the Paris mob. Thus armed, they marched on Versailles in October and brought the king and queen back to the capital, where they remained effective prisoners until their flight to Varennes in June, 1791. (Oil by David, Gamma)

convocation of the Estates General, a body divided into three parts consisting of the clergy, nobility, and commoners.

It was here that all the trouble began. One of Louis's ministers warned him of the potentially disastrous consequences: 'As a Frenchman, I want the Estates General, [but] as a minister I feel bound to tell you that they could destroy your authority.' The political and financial crisis grew throughout 1788, with many army officers discontented at the imposition of new reforms. Things finally came to a head in the spring of 1789 when Louis convened the Estates General. Catastrophic harvest failures had caused a rise in the cost of bread – this in an essentially medieval society still held together by feudal ties and peopled by millions of impoverished peasants and an increasingly discontented urban working class.

The Revolution was unleashed on two very different fronts. The Estates General, which met in May at Versailles, represented political legitimacy, even if they had not been elected by the people; while in Paris, a vast city of 700,000 inhabitants, the crowds had no such claims to power, but would no longer accept disenfranchisement, much less outright tyranny. Events moved swiftly and in June the Estates General – or rather that portion consisting of commoners, known as the Third Estate – declared the creation of a 'National Assembly' and pledged in the famous 'Tennis Court Oath' not to dissolve until a new constitution for the nation had been settled. The nation and not the king was now the supreme authority in the land. The Third Estate regarded itself as the legitimate representative body of the nation. In effect, the king was no longer sovereign.

Louis was not prepared simply to sit back and watch the erosion of royal authority, and while the National Assembly, supported by the people of Paris, might declare the principle of national sovereignty, the king still retained that ultimate instrument of absolutist power: the army. Yet Louis could not depend on this traditional bulwark of the crown. On the contrary, political disaffection in the officer corps was so widespread that it was impossible to rely on the army to confront the National Assembly or, still less, to disperse seething Parisian mobs. Indeed, an overwhelming proportion of the nobles among the Estates General were army officers who actively supported radical political change, and without the army's defection the Revolution would probably never have happened.

Louis recalled elements of the army from the frontiers but feared that they would mutiny if ordered to fire on the people. Worse still, when the French Guards who were garrisoned at Paris began to fraternize with the people, any hopes of relying on them to uphold the royal will evaporated. Then, on the fateful day of 14 July, the mob stormed the Bastille and the Revolution was set on its radical course. But it was not the people alone who captured the great prison-fortress; the French Guards and other mutinous elements of the army provided the military know-how to seize the Bastille, a structure less significant as a bastion of royal power than it was as a storehouse of the weapons needed to arm the new militia, shortly to become the National Guard.

The next day Louis ordered the army to withdraw from Paris and Versailles. Now that the king could no longer depend on his army, the last defense of royal authority had evaporated. One can easily oversimplify the role of the army in explaining the outbreak of the Revolution; it was only one factor among many. Crop failure, food shortages, and bankruptcy also played their part. Yet the army's role was decisive, not only ensuring the survival and expansion of the Revolution at home, but within a few years achieving a succession of military victories. These victories would preserve and consolidate the Revolution, and, in a relatively short space of time, raise French power to heights never dreamt of, much less achieved, under the *ancien régime*.

Opposing strengths

Austria was to become France's most determined continental foe, fighting in both coalitions against the Republic with by far the greatest contribution of forces. Her armies were raised partly by voluntary enlistment and partly by conscription, which in German-speaking areas meant conscription for life. Units were designated 'German', which included men from the Netherlands, Italy and Poland, and 'Hungarian', which included Croatia and Transylvania. Training varied in quality, was often poorly funded and constantly underwent reorganization. Officers were largely drawn from the minor aristocracy, and earned their commissions through social and political connections. Though Austria on paper had an army of nearly 360,000 men, in actual numbers she mobilized only about 230,000 when war began.

As discussed earlier, during the reign of Frederick the Great, Prussia entered the ranks of the Great Powers largely through the remarkable military successes of her king. In the course of two wars against Austria and her allies, Frederick raised the army's reputation and effectiveness to unrivaled heights in Europe. By making maximum use of his relatively scarce resources and small population, by economizing in Spartan style, by a strict system of recruitment and by extolling the virtues of loyalty to state and army, Frederick built an army that was second to none. By the time of his death in 1786, Prussia was the thirteenth largest country in Europe in population and the tenth largest in area, yet possessed the third largest army – the very model of a militarized state which could count on the loyal support of its proud subjects.

However, since the glory days of the Seven Years' War the army had undergone something of a decline, such that by the time Prussia entered the war in 1792 under Frederick William II, it was resting on its laurels and clinging to the tactics of an earlier period. It had fought as recently as 1778 against Austria, and later intervened in Holland in 1787, but with few opportunities for action its deficiencies were not entirely revealed, and the popularly held belief in the superiority of the Prussian army remained the orthodox view of many observers throughout Europe. In contrast to his uncle, Frederick William preferred cooperation with Austria, and thus his kingdom entered the war as Austria's ally with an army numbering a respectable 200,000 men.

When Britain entered the French Revolutionary Wars in 1793 she was unquestionably the world's leading naval power, with 195 ships-of-the-line in commission, 210 frigates, and 256 sloops – a total of over 600 vessels manned by 100,000 men. Emphasis on naval strength had always adversely affected the army, which was small by continental standards. Defeat in the American colonies only a decade earlier had damaged the army's reputation and its leadership left much to be desired. It was not only Britain's navy that was strong. The economy, the product of her booming trade with her far-flung colonies in India, Canada, the West Indies, and elsewhere, as well as with Europe, enabled her to supply her allies with enormous subsidies with which to prosecute their campaigns on the Continent. In 1800 alone the Treasury spent over 7 percent of its total revenue on subsidies, most of it for Austria.

Although Russia did not join the conflict until the formation of the Second Coalition at the end of 1798, her army had recent combat experience in wars with Sweden, Poland, and Turkey, as well as with various peoples on her lengthy frontier. Imperial rule was absolute. The Russian soldier in the ranks was almost invariably illiterate and destitute, and was distinguished by his unquestioning loyalty, high degree of discipline in combat, and his extraordinary ability to endure privation and hardship without complaint.

Vast as the Russian Empire was, stretching from the Baltic to the Ukraine, the Crimea and beyond, its soldiers were principally drawn from the heartland of ancient Great Russia. In theory the army exceeded 400,000 men, including garrison regiments, militia and irregular forces – notably the Cossacks – but in reality its effective strength was much lower. The army and navy were conscripted by imperial levies, of which there were three under Tsar Paul. At the end of Catherine's reign in 1796, Russia had in her regular forces 140,000 infantry (rising to 200,000 by 1800), 30,000 cavalry, and 8,000 in the artillery. Irregular forces were large but of limited value. In any event, Suvorov had only about 20,000 men during his campaign in Switzerland in 1799. Principally a land power, Russia nevertheless possessed a respectable navy operating out of Cronstadt on the Baltic and Sebastopol on the Black Sea. In 1790 she possessed 67 ships-of-the-line, 36 frigates, and 700 sloops, crewed by 21,000 sailors.

Although defeated in the Seven Years' War the French army had regained some of its reputation in America. With monarchist enemies ranged against her in 1792 France burst forth with patriotic fervor with the cry of '*la patrie en danger!*' thus calling forth the massive manpower and financial resources of the nation in a wave of unprecedented nationalist enthusiasm. The officer corps, traditionally dominated by the aristocracy, was by the beginning of the war open to all on merit. However, the flight and purge of royalist officers in the early years of the wars left the army in a pathetic state, and officials found that there was no time to train the large influx of recruits and conscripts. Some even refused to accept the degree of discipline necessary for an effective fighting force. Nevertheless, enough officers and men of the old regular army remained to form a nucleus for the new Republican armies. Without these

veterans, defeat would have been inevitable at the hands of the more professional and better-disciplined armies. Laws formalizing conscription were passed in 1798, requiring all men between the ages of 18 and 40 to register, with those between 18 and 25 liable to be called. Conscription raised vast armies and between January 1791 and July 1799 the French Republic called up 1,570,000 men – an amazing achievement which other nations could not match: they simply did not dare to press into service such a huge proportion of their subjects for fear of political instability.

Since the start of the revolution the army had undergone considerable changes. For example, old regimental titles were abolished and replaced by numbered units, units were increased in size, and large numbers of new battalions were raised. Some of these battalions were of reasonable quality, such as the *Garde Nationale*, while others were poorly trained, often ill-disciplined conscripts and volunteer hordes such as those created by the *levée en masse* in 1793. If they were not quite as drilled and precise as their adversaries, they more than made up for it in élan and devotion to their cause. As one Prussian, Laukhard, noted at the time:

The volunteers were not as straight as a die, as were the Prussians, and were not as polished, well-trained or skilled in handling a gun or marching in step; nor did they know how to tighten their belts around their tunics as the Prussians did, yet they were devoted to the cause they served in body and soul. Nearly all those I encountered at that time knew for whom and for what they were fighting and declared that they were ready to die for the good of their patrie. *The only alternatives they knew were liberty or death.*

The navy consisted of 81 ships-of-the-line, 69 frigates, and 141 sloops, crewed by 78,000 sailors. Numbers can prove deceptive, however: the general state of the ships was poor, dockyards suffered from a shortage of supplies, and the service was generally dogged by an inefficient administration, poor seamanship, defective gunnery, and low morale and discipline.

A clash of ideologies

It might seem logical to presume that the European monarchs, witnessing the fall of the Bastille, the deposing of the French king, and the establishment of constitutional government should immediately have gone to war against the revolutionaries, if only to prevent similar uprisings in their own countries. But it was not to be, largely because of events elsewhere in Europe, particularly in the East. Frederick William, supremely smug from his conquest of Holland in 1787 and already a beneficiary of the first partition of Poland, had his eye on further gains, particularly Danzig and Thorn, while the Austrians and Russians were engaged in conflicts of their own against Sweden and Turkey. The fact that all the continental Great Powers were engaged for two years in intrigues and conflicts in eastern Europe meant that France and its nascent revolution remained undisturbed – indeed almost entirely ignored – by its powerful and otherwise suspicious neighbors.

It is also important to remember that, far from being disturbed by the implications of the French Revolution, many of Britain's leaders and politicians actually welcomed the upheavals in France. When Pitt first heard news of the Revolution while dining with a friend, he 'spoke of it as an event highly favorable to us & indicates a long peace with France.' As the Revolution developed, many British observers suggested that France appeared to be embracing the principles of Britain's own 'Glorious Revolution' of 1688. What better way to maintain good relations than to deal with another constitutional democracy, particularly one distracted from colonial gain and commercial competition by internal political upheaval? In short, a self-obsessed France could hardly threaten British trade or interests abroad.

In fact, none of the continental powers was prepared to lead a counter-revolution. Indeed, the Emperor Joseph was determined to remain neutral, whatever the fate of the French king and the queen, his sister. The Prussians were equally blasé. Catherine of Russia, despite her hostility to the ideas of the Revolution, effectively did nothing, while Charles IV of Spain, cousin of Louis XVI, made vague threats which in reality amounted to nothing more than mere bluster. In any event, he was soon caught up in a nasty disagreement with Britain over far-off Vancouver Island – the Nootka Sound incident – which brought the two countries to the brink of war in 1790. Thus the French Revolutionaries had absolutely no reason to fear intervention by the absolute monarchs. Put in simple terms, in the first two years of the Revolution every potential enemy of significant power had other matters to contend with: in 1787, Turkey was at war with Russia and Austria, and Prussia invaded Holland; in 1788, Sweden and Russia were at war; in 1790, Prussia and Poland came close to war with Austria, and Britain and Spain narrowly escaped conflict; in 1791, Britain and Prussia nearly fought Russia.

How, then, did this atmosphere of complacency and even satisfaction change to one of open hostility? The simple answer is that, by the middle of 1791, all of these conflicts or disputes had been settled, or were on the point of being settled. The most serious of these, in which Russia and Austria were allied against Turkey, ended in August. Now all these countries could consider the problem of France. But the origins of the French Revolutionary Wars also owed much to the vociferous and consistent pleas of royalist émigrés, who tirelessly agitated for armed foreign intervention against the forces of radicalism. The hawkish policies of radical politicians in Paris and the gradually mounting antagonisms of the German monarchies also played a significant role in bringing about war.

Up until the spring of 1792 few obstacles existed to prevent the flight from France of the aristocracy, nobles, clergy, and army officers. Large numbers left, swelling the population of disaffected expatriates longing for a return to the old order. They were right to leave, for their lives and livelihoods were under grave threat and the political changes forced upon them were naturally quite intolerable to them when compared to the life of unchecked privilege that they had previously enjoyed for so long. The leading émigré was the king's younger brother, the Comte d'Artois, who left France soon after the fall of the Bastille and became the focal point for dispossessed aristocrats. From their base at Turin, Artois and his adherents established a committee which throughout 1789–90 produced plans to extricate the King from Paris, establish counter-revolutionary insurrections inside France, and secure foreign aid in a royalist crusade to crush the Revolution and re-establish legitimate Bourbon rule.

Yet all such plans failed completely, for they were unable to attain the aid necessary from powerful foreign governments without which any hopes of a return to absolute rule were illusory. Although Austria seemed the natural ally of the émigrés – after all, Marie Antoinette was sister to Joseph II – the fact remained that from the outbreak of the Revolution until 1792 the Habsburg monarchy never showed much enthusiasm for the émigré cause. Indeed, Joseph had demanded their departure from his domains in the Netherlands, and when his brother Leopold succeeded to the imperial throne at the beginning of 1790 he showed little interest in the cause of restoring Bourbon rule on its previous footing.

In any event, the pressing internal problems that Leopold confronted necessarily took precedence over foreign affairs: rebellion in the Austrian Netherlands and near-revolt in Hungary, together with more moderate, but nevertheless widespread, dissent across Habsburg domains. These domestic problems were compounded by

failures in the war against the Ottoman Empire. Thus, in the course of his two years in power (1790–92), Leopold chose to placate internal opposition and implement reforms rather than confront revolutionary France.

Yet if Leopold's conduct exasperated émigrés for a time, French domestic events gradually altered his views and, with them, his policies. Louis's flight from Paris to Varennes in June 1791 was important in prompting Austrian intervention. Louis had consistently rejected proposals to leave France and return at the front of an army determined on re-establishing Bourbon rule. Duty to the nation and to himself as sovereign – however restricted his political role had become – encouraged him to remain in Paris. But by the spring of 1791 the King had come round to the idea, for by then it had become all too clear that the Revolution was no mere passing phase and that the concessions now forced on him were only going to increase in the future. Now persuaded that the only sensible measure was to flee the country to secure foreign aid, Louis made his historic escape from the capital, only to be arrested at Varennes and returned to Paris a prisoner. The suspension of his royal powers soon followed and all government matters were now the responsibility of the Constituent Assembly.

The King's attempt to leave France had far-reaching consequences, triggering fears inside the country that foreign armies would soon be on the march to save the captive sovereign. Vigorous military measures were undertaken and the widespread belief that foreign intervention was only a matter of time began to affect the political scene throughout the country. The King's arrest had still more significance abroad, for throughout Europe both at court and among the populace there emerged a groundswell of sympathetic support for the French royal family and a sense of apprehension for their safety. Such sentiment was encouraged by the constant calls for aid from Marie Antoinette. Action soon resulted: in July 1791, Leopold approached the other crowned heads with a proposal for a joint declaration demanding the release of the

French royal family, the 'Padua Circular'. This did not amount to a threat of war – which Leopold did not seek – but rather a demonstration of royalist unity meant to overawe the Republican government.

In fact, there was no unified opposition to the French revolutionary movement at the courts of Europe, though each of them provided substantial financial assistance to the émigré cause. Tsarina Catherine adamantly opposed the Revolution, but her foreign policy remained focused on acquiring territory at the expense of Poland and Turkey, both weak and easy prey. Sweden, under Gustavus III, wholeheartedly embraced military action against the revolutionaries, but his country's geographical isolation and meager resources precluded any unilateral intervention on his part. In any event, Gustavus was assassinated in March 1792. The Prussian king repeatedly declared his desire for a military solution to French internal upheaval and the threats which revolutionary ideas posed abroad. Nonetheless, like Catherine, Frederick William had an eye on Polish land and was not prepared to fight unaided. Thus, in the summer of 1791, in spite of growing antagonism within the courts of several capitals, the likelihood of joint military intervention in France remained slight.

That situation soon took a decisive turn, however, for since Leopold had assumed the Imperial throne, Austro-Prussian relations – traditionally tense and occasionally outwardly hostile – had improved considerably. This made possible a joint declaration by the respective sovereigns, issued at Pillnitz on 27 August 1791, which expressed their anxieties over Louis's predicament and their hope that the leading royal houses of Europe would make a joint effort to assist him. Though outwardly threatening, it was not a general call to arms and in any event did not commit Austria and Prussia to anything without the cooperation of other powers. It aimed to

put an end to the anarchy in the interior of France, to stop the attacks carried on against the throne and the altar, to re-establish the legal power, to restore to the king the security and liberty of which he is deprived, and to put him in a position to exercise the legitimate authority which is his due.

No such support was forthcoming, and Pillnitz remained for a time nothing more than bluster and intimidation.

However ineffective the declaration appeared for the moment, it nevertheless added to the general sense of impending danger within France. As the year progressed, moreover, the prospect of war became an ever more attractive option for those politicians in Paris who viewed it as an opportunity to attain their own specific aims. This was particularly the case among the war party under the leadership of Jacques-Pierre Brissot, whose popularity continued to rise as the new year began. His followers, the 'Brissotins' or 'Girondins', held an aggressive stance in the Legislative Assembly. The 37-year-old Brissot, an unsuccessful writer with a grudge against the ruling establishment, had been one of the first to call for the abolition of the monarchy. Brissot was not alone. By the winter of 1791–92 the Jacobins could more than match the Girondins for radicalism. Yet as a speech delivered on 26 December by Gensonné, one of Brissot's colleagues, shows, the Girondins were exceptionally provocative as they stood: 'The common enemy is at the gates of the city; a general assault threatens us; so now there can be no more beating about the bush; let us rush to the breach; we must defend our ramparts or bury ourselves beneath their ruins.'

A fortnight later Guadet stood before the Assembly and raised the members to fever pitch in a dramatic foretaste of the hysteria which was to engulf France during the Reign of Terror two years later. 'Gentlemen,' he declared earnestly, 'let us make known to all these German princes that the French nation has decided to maintain its constitution in its entirety; we shall die here.' His words were met with wild applause as the members rose in acclamation with cries of 'Yes, we swear it!' Waving their hats in the air and with arms outstretched, the deputies, government ministers, ushers, and those throwing the public galleries shouted a common oath: 'We shall live in freedom or we shall die, the constitution or death!' Amidst the tumult Guadet concluded his speech in words calculated to bring the house down: 'In a word, let us mark out in advance a place for traitors, and that place will be on the scaffold!' The message was clear: the Republic must have war; a war with total victory or total defeat. The nation was to live free or die in its defense, while those at home who threatened France from within would be crushed.

At the same time, those at the opposite end of the political spectrum – the monarchy and its traditional ally, the aristocracy – increasingly viewed war as an answer to their rapidly declining political fortunes. Into this cauldron of hostility was thrown the still active efforts of the émigrés to restore the status quo, and however little their efforts may have as yet achieved, their very existence assumed an importance out of all proportion to the actual danger to the Revolution that they presented. The recent growth of an émigré presence in the Rhineland, an area used as the springboard for the émigrés' subversive schemes, naturally raised concerns for the Republican government, ever vigilant for evidence of counter-revolutionary enemies within and without France.

Artois and his adherents amounted to a sort of royalist government in exile, based at Koblenz; although their influence in foreign courts was minimal, seen together with the Declaration of Pillnitz, the émigrés were erroneously assumed to be a real and powerful threat to the Revolution. In addition to receiving large amounts of financial aid, Artois could boast of a respectably sized émigré army in the Rhineland. The threat posed by such forces was negligible in military terms, but the very presence of this émigré army caused widespread alarm in France, where war fever was spreading.

Austria was not only pressured by the émigrés but also miscalculated the situation by adopting an increasingly threatening attitude designed to intimidate but not provoke the republican government in Paris, Leopold paradoxically achieved the reverse of his intentions. Hoping to lend weight to the power of the moderates in Paris, he in fact increased the power of the radicals. Thus was created a vicious circle: increasing French fears of émigré activity on their borders and the apparently menacing posture of Austria and Prussia gave impetus to the general atmosphere of fear and the prospect of not only counter-revolution, but also armed foreign intervention.

Events took on a new momentum with 1 March 1792, and the succession of Francis. Consistently unwilling to embrace the more bellicose views of the Prussian king, the princes of the Empire, and the émigrés, Leopold had preferred merely to pressure France rather than openly threaten her with force. True, he had shown greater support for the restoration to power of Louis XVI – briefly suspended by the National Assembly after Varennes before moderates reinstated him in September 1791 – than most other crowned heads, yet Leopold's death ushered in an entirely new Habsburg attitude toward foreign affairs. Leopold had acted with caution and restraint; Francis tended more toward belligerence. The hawkish elements of the court grew in influence while the new cabinet, particularly with the replacement of the more pacific chancellor, Kaunitz, opened the way for an altogether more hostile policy toward revolutionary France. The road to war was now free of its former obstacles.

OPPOSITE On the eve of the French Revolutionary Wars the European continent contained about 180 million people, most of whom still lived under feudal conditions within the realms of a sovereign or prince endowed with substantial – if not autocratic – power over his subjects. Representative institutions with more than simply a token political role were rare, and even in Britain the franchise extended only to men of sufficient property or financial means. In the realm of power politics five powers stood above the rest: Britain, France, Austria, Russia and Prussia. Austria was a natural target for those revolutionaries looking to export their creed: to the north lay the Austrian Netherlands; to the east the Holy Roman Empire, over whom the Habsburgs traditionally exercised their not inconsiderable power and influence, and to the south lay Italy, another region with strong Habsburg connections.

Europe in 1792

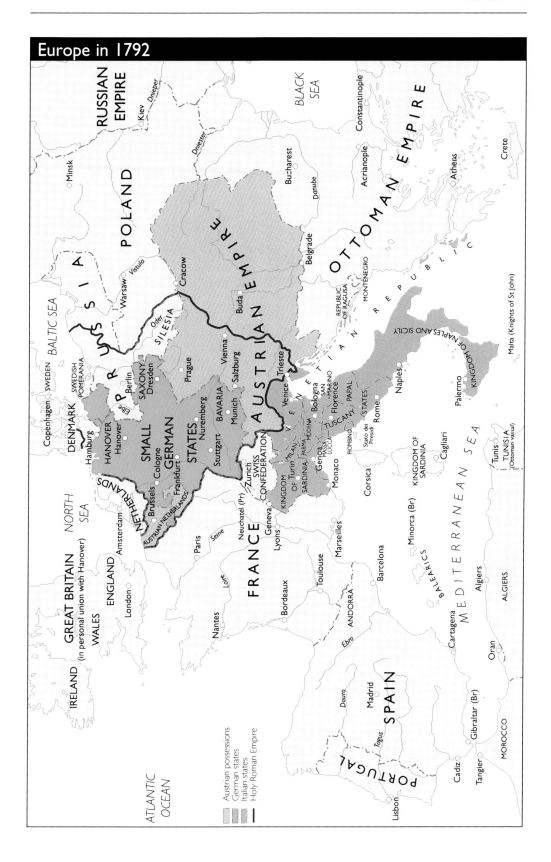

Legend:
- Austrian possessions
- German states
- Italian states
- ▬ Holy Roman Empire

ATLANTIC OCEAN

IRELAND

GREAT BRITAIN (in personal union with Hanover)

WALES

ENGLAND

London

NORTH SEA

DENMARK

Copenhagen

SWEDEN

BALTIC SEA

SWEDISH POMERANIA

RUSSIAN EMPIRE

Minsk

Kiev   Dnieper

Dniester

POLAND

Warsaw   Vistula

Cracow

P R U S S I A

Berlin

Hamburg

Hanover

HANOVER

SMALL GERMAN STATES

Cologne

Frankfurt

Brussels

AUSTRIAN NETHERLANDS

NETHERLANDS

Amsterdam

Elbe

SAXONY

Dresden

Oder

SILESIA

Prague

Nuremberg

Stuttgart

BAVARIA

Munich

Salzburg

Vienna

Buda

AUSTRIAN EMPIRE

Trieste

Venice

V E N E T I A N

Milan

KINGDOM OF Turin

SARDINIA

PARMA

MODENA

MASSA

LUCCA

Genoa

Monaco

PIOMBINO

TUSCANY

Florence

SAN MARINO

Bologna

PAPAL STATES

Rome

Stato dei Presidi

KINGDOM OF NAPLES AND SICILY

Naples

Palermo

OTTOMAN EMPIRE

Bucharest

Danube

Belgrade

REPUBLIC OF RAGUSA

MONTENEGRO

R E P U B L I C

Constantinople

Acrianople

Athens

Crete

BLACK SEA

Malta (Knights of St John)

Corsica

KINGDOM OF SARDINIA

Cagliari

Tunis

TUNISIA (Ottoman vassal)

MEDITERRANEAN SEA

Zurich

SWISS CONFEDERATION

Geneva

Neuchatel (Pr)

Lyons

Paris   Seine

Loire

Nantes

Bordeaux

Toulouse

Marseilles

FRANCE

ANDORRA

Barcelona

Minorca (Br)

BALEARICS

Algiers

ALGIERS

Ebro

SPAIN

Madrid

Douro

Cartagena

Oran

MOROCCO

PORTUGAL

Tagus

Lisbon

Cadiz

Tangier

Gibraltar (Br)

As politicians in Paris were rightly perceiving the changing mood in Vienna, they were growing more vocal and bellicose themselves. The new foreign minister, Charles François Dumouriez, came to office from relative obscurity amidst the growing war fever. Long hostile to Austria, Dumouriez demanded immediate military action. War now seemed inevitable. Indeed, it was not long in coming: on 20 April, France formally declared war on Austria. '*The National Assembly,*' the declaration of war ran,

*declares that the French nation, faithful to the principles consecrated in the constitution, **not to undertake any war with a view to making conquest, and never to employ its forces against the liberty of any people**, takes arms only to maintain its liberty and its independence.*

That the war which it is forced to sustain is not a war of nation against nation, but the just defense of a free people against the unjust aggression of a king.

That the French will never confound their brothers with their real enemies; that they will neglect nothing in order to alleviate the scourge of war, to spare and preserve property, and to cause to return upon those alone, who shall league themselves against its liberties, all the miseries inseparable from war.

Little did anyone know that this war – which all sides believed would be short – would eventually engulf all of Europe in more than two decades of conflict.

Neither side bore sole responsibility for the war. The conflict cannot be said to have originated either exclusively in Paris or in Vienna. It was not only kings and politicians who shaped foreign policy; prevailing views among the general populace in both capitals played their role. In the end both sides sought war, but their objectives proved very different. Austria, joined shortly by Prussia

on 21 May, wished to restore the old order in France, whereas for the revolutionaries this was to be an ideological struggle between a free people and the tyranny of monarchical rule. This had been the philosophy so stridently advocated by Brissot since the autumn of 1791. Toward this end the revolutionaries were confident in their hopes of seeing a general rising of the minority nationalities of the Habsburg Empire: they were to be sorely disappointed.

Those powers ranged against France clung steadfastly to a policy more than merely ideological: there were distinct territorial gains to be made, a wholly realistic aim when one considers the Allies' complete confidence in the superiority of their professional, highly trained, highly disciplined armies over the rabble that appeared to them to constitute the forces of the Republic. It was therefore not surprising that the Allies did not yet appreciate the immense threat to the political stability of Europe's monarchies posed by the armies marching in the name of 'the People', for those armies were as yet untested. They could hardly then know – and indeed it would be to the astonishment of all – that the revolutionary armies would, despite some serious setbacks, achieve remarkable triumphs in the field between 1793 and 1795, rapidly annexing neighboring territories in great swathes never even imagined – much less achieved – by Louis XIV or Louis XV. Nor could the Allies have dared to imagine the full horror that lay ahead for them: seemingly unstoppable revolutionary forces carrying with them the banner of *liberté, egalité et fraternilé* across western and central Europe, challenging the very legitimacy of monarchical rule. Only then was the war perceived as the truly grave threat to European political and social stability that it actually was.

The first and second coalitions

The War of the First Coalition, 1792–97

The Campaign of 1792

The French Revolutionary Wars were divided into two distinct periods, organized around the War of the First Coalition (1792–97) and that of the Second Coalition (1798–1802), each with its own combination of European powers. The fervor of revolutionary ideology in France, together with the revulsion that it inspired abroad, brought France into open conflict with Austria and Prussia, soon to be joined by various other states. The Allies expected a quick and decisive victory. Once across the Rhine they expected to brush aside the poorly equipped amateurish forces sent to meet them. At the end of a decade of continuous fighting, the French Revolutionary Wars left France in a far stronger position than she had begun them, controlling not only the so-called 'natural' frontiers of the Rhine, the Alps, and the Pyrenees, but exercising considerable influence over her satellite states in the Low Countries, western Germany, Italy, and Switzerland. These achievements, though relatively swiftly attained, were made only after fighting on an unprecedented scale, in many separate theaters of war and under very different geographical conditions.

When hostilities began in April 1792, France deployed her armies along all her borders. To the north, two officers distinguished by their previous service in the War of American Independence, Generals Rochambeau and Lafayette, with about 50,000 men each, held positions extending from the northern coast to the Ardennes. A somewhat smaller army under General Luckner stood near the Rhine further south. Fifty thousand men under Montesquieu

occupied the border with Piedmont, on the south coast. Each of these armies was understrength and suffered from poor discipline and disorganization.

Fighting began when French forces invaded the Austrian Netherlands (modern Belgium), where, at Valenciennes, the Republicans overcame all resistance in the first action of the war. Further south, along the Rhine, however, the Austrians and Prussians were aiming directly for Paris itself. The prospect of invasion had a profound effect in the French capital, where the National Assembly decreed that every citizen was to come forward in defense of the Republic, while radical politicians moved closer to deposing the King. On 24 July Prussia, together with a number of lesser German states, formally joined Austria's cause by declaring war on France.

On 1 August the Allies issued the Brunswick Manifesto, a statement that proved immensely counter-productive since it inadvertently fanned the flames of revolutionary fervor in France. While it was meant to be an ominous warning of punishment which would cow the French, as well as being a pledge to protect Louis XVI, it played into the hands of French propagandists who presented it as a dire threat to the nation's existence. If the Tuileries were attacked, the Brunswick Manifesto said,

if the least violence or outrage be offered to their Majesties, the king, queen and royal family, if their preservation and their liberty be not immediately provided for, they [the Allies] will exact an exemplary and ever-memorable vengeance, by delivering the city of Paris over to a military execution and to complete ruin, and the rebels guilty of these outrages to the punishments they shall have deserved.

Parisians bid farewell to the National Guard, September 1792. Scenes like these took place all over France: soldiers leaving for the front kiss their sweethearts and receive bouquets from enthusiastic ladies lining the streets while men cheer and raise or throw their hats into the air. 'Every citizen should be a soldier,' proclaimed one revolutionary, 'and every soldier should be a citizen.' (Print after Coginet, Roger-Viollet)

Received in Paris on 3 August, it caused widespread public demonstrations and the imprisonment of the King, who was now sovereign in name only. The determination to repel the enemy grew enormously and volunteer enlistments rose at an astonishing pace.

Initially the army of the Duke of Brunswick met little resistance in its August advance on the French capital. In leisurely fashion he took the fortresses at Longwy and Verdun before proceeding through the Argonne forest. Opposing him was the Army of the Centre under General François Kellermann, joined by part of the Army of the North under General Charles Dumouriez. Together the Generals could deploy 36,000 men of dubious quality compared to the

34,000 professional troops under Brunswick. At last, on September 20, the two armies met at a position prepared by the French at Valmy. Both sides opened a cannonade until 1 pm, when the Prussian guns fell silent and their infantry, arrayed in two lines, marched forward in attack. Kellermann seized the moment: raising his hat on his sword he cried '*Vive la Nation!*' and thousands of troops answered back in a great surge of patriotic enthusiasm. To the astonishment of the French, Brunswick halted his attack and withdrew – and he did not stop until he had gone back across the Rhine. Goethe, who was present with the allied army, rightly perceived the great historical significance of the French victory, for not only did it save Paris, it saved the Revolution itself. 'From here and today,' he told his colleagues, 'there begins a new epoch in the history of the world, and you can say that you were there.'

On the southern front Montesquieu's army invaded Piedmont and Savoy, capturing Nice in the process. Dumouriez, for his part, made progress in the north. On his approach the Austrians raised the siege of Lille and made camp for the winter at Jemappes, just over the Belgian frontier. Now was the time for Dumouriez to strike. While Austrian and Prussian attention was diverted by matters in Poland, where the Eastern powers were arranging the second partition of that unfortunate country, Dumouriez launched another, more powerful invasion, this time with 40,000 men and 100 guns, defeating the 13,000 Austrians at Jemappes on 6 November.

The battle was a turning point in the war, for the French followed up by taking Brussels 10 days later, and sent a squadron up the Scheldt to besiege Antwerp. Significantly, the French had now adopted new tactics and displayed a thirst for the offensive, or élan, which was to serve them well over the next several years. Meanwhile, on the Rhine front, neither side had gained the upper hand. General Custine took Mainz but penetrated into Germany only as far as Frankfurt. Nevertheless, by the end of 1792, republican armies had preserved the nation and, moreover, sat ominously on the borders of Holland, while at home the Revolution had taken a more radical turn. A new government, the National Convention, came to power and promptly abolished the monarchy.

This, together with a French declaration on 16 November that opened the Scheldt Estuary to international shipping (in overt violation of existing treaties which guaranteed Holland sole control), led Britain to make war preparations. British security rested on the premise that no great maritime power held control of the Channel ports. Britain was right to be concerned, for Dumouriez planned to invade the Dutch Republic in the spring. In Paris Anglophobia was growing rapidly, particularly within the National Assembly.

The so-called 'Edict of Fraternity', issued on 19 November, gave further alarm in Britain, for it was an open invitation for radicals across Europe – and specifically within the small German states of the Holy

Valmy, 20 September 1792. In one of history's most decisive battles, the Duke of Brunswick made two half-hearted advances against Dumouriez and Kellermann before acknowledging his numerical inferiority and declaring: 'We shall not strike here.' French morale soared. 'The French Revolutionaries have come through their baptism of fire,' noted one Prussian officer. 'They expected more from us. Now we have fallen in their estimation, but they have risen. We have lost more than a battle. Our credibility is gone.' (Gamma)

Roman Empire – to overthrow their governments, whether or not those governments were then hostile to France. The French could hardly have produced a more provocative document:

The National Convention declares, in the name of the French nation, that it will grant fraternity and assistance to all peoples who wish to recover their liberty, and instructs the Executive Power to give the necessary orders to the generals to grant assistance to these peoples and to defend those citizens who have been – or may be – persecuted for their attachment to the cause of liberty.

The critical point came on 21 January 1793. The execution of Louis XVI caused outrage throughout Europe, including Britain, where the government had already begun discussing military plans with Austrian and Prussian officials. Just 10 days later, on 31 January, the National Assembly formally annexed Belgium, and it declared war on Britain and Holland the next day. The power of the Allies' coalition was enormously increased with the additional military, naval, and above all financial resources of Britain, who began to use her diplomatic influence to draw in other members. Naples and Portugal soon joined the ranks of the Allies, followed by Spain, on whom France declared war on 7 March. To these Sweden and Russia gave their sympathy, if not their practical support.

The Campaign of 1793

France faced a whole host of threats in the spring of 1793: to the south Spain could mount an attack across the Pyrenees; Austrian and Italian troops were preparing for the spring campaign season near Nice; a multinational army under British command was being readied for operations in Flanders in conjunction with Habsburg forces; and the Allies now boasted an army of 120,000 men along the Rhine. These combined forces numbered nearly 350,000 men, while in France civil and political instability, workers' strikes, and

administrative collapse left the armies of the Republic lacking in supplies and pay and suffering from low morale. In theory they numbered 270,000, but the true figure must have been considerably lower, and with morale at its lowest point there was no telling what the next season of campaigning would bring. To make matters worse, France had now also to contend with the powerful Royal Navy, which was reckoned by all more than a match for its French counterpart. With France already on the verge of bankruptcy, the prospect of losing her colonies and having her commerce swept from the seas must have seemed like a nightmare.

The French duly invaded Holland in the middle of February, but the Allies were meanwhile launching their own offensive with 40,000 Austrians under the Prince of Saxe-Coburg, who crossed the Meuse to retake Belgium. On the Rhine, Brunswick returned with 60,000 Prussians to besiege Custine in Mainz, but neither of their two operations was vigorously pressed. Indeed, the allied campaign in Flanders stumbled along without any rush to reach the French frontier. Adhering to the strategies of previous wars, the forces of the coalition instead chose to spend the summer consolidating their ground by laying siege to the cities of Valenciennes, Condé, and Mainz.

Nevertheless, the French under General Francisco de Miranda suffered defeat at Maastricht on 6 March, while on the 18th, at Neerwinden, Dumouriez launched eight separate columns totaling 45,000 men against Saxe-Coburg in an attempt to turn his left. The French columns were defeated in detail, rapidly putting paid to French plans of swift conquest. The Austrians retook Brussels, and Dumouriez, unwilling to face the inevitable backlash in Paris where his Jacobin political enemies demanded blood, defected to the enemy on 5 April. Custine, who ultimately replaced him, was defeated at the besieged city of Valenciennes on 21–23 May, and fell victim to the ruthless Committee of Public Safety in Paris, the main instrument of the Reign of Terror (a sort of revolutionary dictatorship led by

Maximilien Robespierre). Custine was sent to the guillotine, setting a chilling precedent for many other generals who would either fail on the battlefield or whose loyalties to the Republic would come under suspicion. Saxe-Coburg duly followed up his success by taking Condé on 10 July and Valenciennes on the 29th.

While the Terror sought to cleanse France of its internal enemies – real and imagined – the nation was in an increasingly dangerous position, with fighting along the Pyrenees and, from August, serious royalist counter-revolutions under way in the Vendée, Lyon, and Toulon. An Anglo-Spanish fleet under Admiral Lord Hood appeared off Toulon, disembarked troops for its defense against republican forces, and prepared to burn or capture the French fleet sitting at anchor. The British were also active to the north, dispatching an Anglo-Hanoverian expedition under the Duke of York to Flanders, where it invested Dunkirk and linked forces with the Austrians to the east. Elsewhere, with low morale among both their leaders and men, French forces along the Rhine could not hope to stop the allied advance from the east that recaptured Mainz in August. These were dark times indeed for France, a country now apparently on the point of collapse.

Fortunes shifted, however, as a result of faulty allied strategy and wrangling among the various governments. The new offensive in Flanders failed to concentrate its forces, dividing them instead between the British, who marched on Dunkirk, and the Austrians, who laid siege to Quesnoy. These forces now confronted French armies that were newly enlarged, well led, and encouraged by the far-reaching reforms instituted by Lazare Carnot, the new War Minister. Later dubbed the 'Organizer of Victory', Carnot was instrumental in formulating the famous *levée en masse*, decreed on 23 August, by which the Republic ordered the conscription of the entire male population. *From this moment until that in which the enemy shall have been driven from the soil of the Republic*, ran one of the Revolution's greatest documents,

all Frenchmen are in permanent requisition for the service of the armies. The young men

shall go to battle; the married men shall forge arms and transport provisions; the women shall make tents and clothing and shall serve in the hospitals; the children shall turn old linen into lint; the aged shall betake themselves to the public places in order to arouse the courage of the warriors and preach the hatred of kings and the unity of the Republic.

Within a matter of weeks the tireless Carnot had raised an astonishing 14 new armies.

On the very day this call to arms was issued, Marseilles fell to republican forces. The following two months witnessed a series of great battlefield achievements. On 8 September the French counter-attacked the Duke of York at Hondschoote, near Dunkirk. The new commander in Flanders, General Houchard, flung his 42,000 men forward in a series of madcap and uncoordinated assaults. The sheer size of his army gave the Anglo-Hanoverians, though they were better trained and more experienced, no choice but to retreat and abandon their siege train. Hondschoote ended the revolutionary armies' series of defeats and turned the tide in their favor once again. The French armies went forward, bent on further victories and

William Pitt addressing the House of Commons, 1793. His early prediction that the Revolution would bring Britain 15 years of peace was entirely misplaced, though not, at the time, inconceivable. After the strategic and ideological threat posed by revolutionary France became clear, Pitt became a staunch advocate for war and was instrumental in establishing the First and Second Coalitions, which he backed with only limited, often unsuccessful, military expeditions but a significant naval and financial commitment. (Ann Ronan Picture Library)

OPPOSITE Shifting fortunes and policies inevitably meant that nations entered and left the conflict at different times:

1. **France** At war, April 1792–October 1797; hostilities continued against Britain and Portugal.
2. **Austria** Against France, April 1792–October 1797.
3. **Britain** Against France, February 1793–March 1802.
4. **Prussia** Against France, June 1792–April 1795.
5. **Holland** Against France, February 1793–1795; thereafter a French ally as the Batavian Republic.
6. **Spain** Against France, August 1792–July 1795; French ally against Britain, October 1796–March 1802.
7. **Portugal** Against France, March 1793–1801; against Spain, France's ally, 1801.
8. **Small German states of the Holy Roman Empire** Baden, 1793–96; Bavaria, 1792; Hanover, 1792–95; Hessel-Cassel, 1792–95; Hesse-Darmstadt, 1792–1799; Saxony, 1792–96; Wurttemberg, 1792–97.
9. **Northern and central Italian states** Initiated war against France or attacked or forcibly occupied by her: Sardinia, 1792–96; Parma, 1796; Genoese Republic, 1792; Venetian Republic, 1796.
10. **Naples** Against France, 1793–96.

Belligerent powers in the first coalition

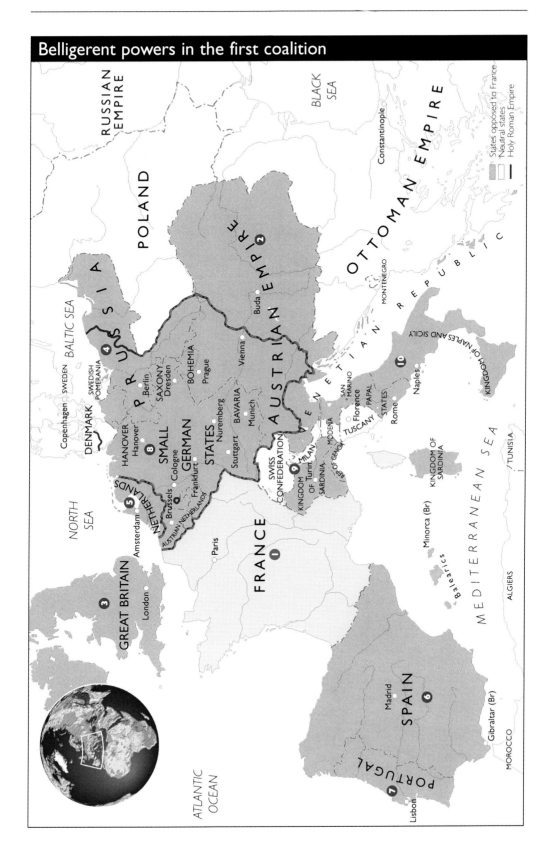

Lazare Carnot. As War Minister from August 1793 Carnot was instrumental in establishing a host of fundamental army reforms which contributed greatly to success in the field, most notably the *levée en masse*, which swelled the ranks of the armies to unprecedented levels. Extremely diligent and hard-working, Carnot oversaw the reorganization of the infantry at demi-brigade level and the armies at corps level, improved mobility for the artillery, introduced the use of semaphore and oversaw large-scale factory production of arms and materiel. (Ann Ronan Picture Library)

further conquests. Only five days later Houchard crushed the Prince of Orange, whose forces fled in disorder.

Despite these successes, the unfortunate French general went to the guillotine for failing to drive the Austrians out of eastern France. He was succeeded by General Jean-Baptiste Jourdan. Jourdan, accompanied in the field by Carnot, sought to relieve Maubeuge, which was being besieged by Saxe-Coburg's 30,000 Austrians. The two-day Battle of Wattignies resulted. On 15 October the better-trained Austrians held off the attacks of 50,000 determined yet less disciplined Republican troops. On the following day Jourdan turned his opponent's left flank,

obliging him to raise the siege of Maubeuge and withdraw eastward. Thus, by the end of autumn, nearly all allied forces had been driven from northeastern France. Growing numbers and a determined spirit to prevail were now bringing success for the revolutionary armies which, beginning with Hondschoote, could now maneuver in battle rather than simply charge in headlong assault.

The Republic enjoyed further successes on other fronts. On the Rhine the Allies retreated to the east side of the river after their reverse at the Geisberg on 26 December. In October Kellermann had driven out the Piedmontese army from the newly conquered French territory of Savoy. Despite the French defeat at Truillas on 22 September, republican forces had held the Spanish front at a time when Spain was beginning to lose interest in the war. In the meantime, the civil war within France against the royalist counter-revolution had also turned in the Republic's favor: Lyon was retaken on 20 October and after bloody resistance and a campaign of exceptionally brutal repression, the revolt in the Vendée was finally subdued.

At sea, although Britain had failed to engage a French fleet, it will be recalled that she had sent an expedition to Toulon where the royalist populace found itself besieged by a frenzied Republican army. Hood managed to destroy much of the French fleet in the harbor but the Allies wrangled over strategy, the Spanish failed to cooperate as intended, and the expedition failed to stem the Republican onslaught. The city fell to the revolutionaries' vengeance on 19 December. The government in Paris had decreed the death of its citizens as traitors, and thousands, including women and children, were murdered in cold blood.

By coincidence the siege brought two rising stars to the scene of action: the 35-year-old Captain Horatio Nelson and the 24-year-old Captain Napoleon Bonaparte. As commander of the artillery at Toulon, Bonaparte played a decisive role in the recapture of the city. Once in possession of the heights above the harbor he directed the bombardment that drove off the allied fleet. Nelson, the diminutive captain of the *Agamemnon*, also served for a time at Toulon. Supremely self-confident to the point of arrogance, he relished a good fight and predicted for himself a great future, boasting to a British diplomat, 'I am, now, only a captain; but I will, if I live, be at the top of the tree.' Elsewhere at sea, while Britain's policy of blockade enabled her to concentrate on French trade and colonies, it was soon clear that neither fleet actions nor blockade could, without greater success on land, bring the revolutionary government to heel.

The Campaigns of 1794–95

By 1794, the reforms introduced by Carnot were rapidly yielding returns. Conscription on an unprecedented scale had raised 1.5 million men since the introduction of the *levée en masse*, and the nation now had in the field 15 armies totaling nearly 800,000 men. The armies of the Ardennes and the North, stationed in the northeast, numbered almost 300,000; the armies of the Rhine and of the Moselle had 200,000 men; about 120,000 stood along the Pyrenees and the Italian frontier; and the Army of the Interior had a respectable 85,000 men. Carnot's strategy required that these vast new armies were to depend on living off the land. Keeping them on foreign soil thus became a priority for the French government, which was concerned about the nation's resources being exhausted and about the potential political threat they might pose in the hands of a renegade commander.

While the ranks of the revolutionary armies had swelled beyond anything previously seen in modern war, allied numbers and coordination were rapidly declining. With only 430,000 men to deploy on all fronts, their forces of 180,000 in Flanders and 145,000 on the Rhine were now for the first time inferior to the numbers opposing them. Both Austria and Prussia became increasingly distracted by affairs in Poland. Russia's intervention in the civil war there gave them cause for concern. Continued military setbacks and the

Kléber fought successfully in the Vendée in 1793–94 and at the pivotal battle of Fleurus, but he is most associated with the campaign in the Middle East, where he became C-in-C after Bonaparte's departure. The abortive Convention of El Arish failed to deliver his army safe passage home and despite preserving Cairo by his victory over the Turks at Heliopolis, he was murdered in June 1800. (Ann Ronan Picture Library)

influence of republicanism in the politics of the smaller coalition states were causing them to reconsider their participation in the alliance. Britain meanwhile struggled to keep the alliance alive through diplomacy and subsidies. The example of Prussia best illustrates the lack of cohesion of the alliance: its promise to provide an army of over 60,000 men for the coming spring campaign was never fulfilled. Austria, for her part, agreed to cooperate in an offensive through Flanders at the same time.

On 6 January 1794, the Duke of Brunswick resigned as commander on the Rhine. Within a fortnight the French had seized his last position on the west bank of the river. Neither side in fact took the offensive and, apart from the arrest and imprisonment of General Hoche, who criticized this inactivity, nothing of consequence occurred on this front. Instead, the principal events of the season's campaigning took place in Italy and in Flanders, where the Allies' offensive foundered as soon as it reached the first fortified position. In stark contrast, in April the new commander of the Army of the North, General

Jean-Charles Pichegru, began a series of strikes at numerous points along the front which resulted in triumphs at Courtrai on 11 May and at Tourcoing on the 18th. The combined Austrian, Hanoverian, and British force under Saxe-Coburg was thus forced eastwards, leaving the main British contingent under the Duke of York in a vulnerable position around Tournai. There, on the 23rd, the rival armies of about 50,000 men each fought an indecisive action before separating.

In June, leading a new combined force known as the Army of the Sambre and Meuse (which numbered about 80,000), Jourdan proceeded toward the allied left at the Sambre and was confronted at Fleurus on the 26th by Saxe-Coburg, with 52,000 men. The Allies attacked the French and achieved initial success until stopped by counterattacks led by Kléber and Jourdan. The following day Saxe-Coburg retreated to the Dutch border, together with York's contingent, allowing Pichegru and Jourdan to follow up and join forces. The French

Napoleon Bonaparte in 1796. A student of artillery, at Toulon in 1793 he rose from captain to brigadier-general on the strength of his successful plan for recapturing the city. He went on to perform well in Italy in 1794 but his destiny was not truly shaped until he used his cannon to save the government from an angry mob in 1795. In gratitude he was appointed C-in-C to the Army of Italy, the post in which he established himself as a great military commander. (Engraving by W. Greatbach, Ann Ronan Picture Library)

Horatio Nelson. Patriotic and brave, yet excessively vain and self-promoting, Nelson fought in numerous sieges, single ship actions, raids, and fleet engagements. His significant contribution at St. Vincent and his later victories at the Nile and at Copenhagen made him a national icon years before Trafalgar. By the end of the Revolutionary Wars he had been blinded in his right eye, had lost his right arm to amputation and had suffered a serious injury to his head. (Ann Ronan Picture Library)

retook Brussels on 10 July and entered Antwerp on the 27th. The Austrians never subsequently regained control over Belgium.

On the Italian front, advancing French troops had by May made possible renewed trade connections with Genoa, while a French offensive in November drove the Spanish back across the frontier over the eastern Pyrenees. The French offensive on the Rhine, concentrated in the Vosges Mountains, had meanwhile forced Austrian and Prussian troops to the eastern side.

Further afield, a British expedition to seize French West Indian possessions was dogged by tropical disease and the arrival of enemy reinforcements. Admiral Sir John Jervis took Martinique, St Lucia, and Guadeloupe in April, but the French managed to recover them all. The Royal Navy did manage to fight one major action, known as the Glorious First of June, between Lord Howe, with 26 ships-of-

Operations in the West Indies

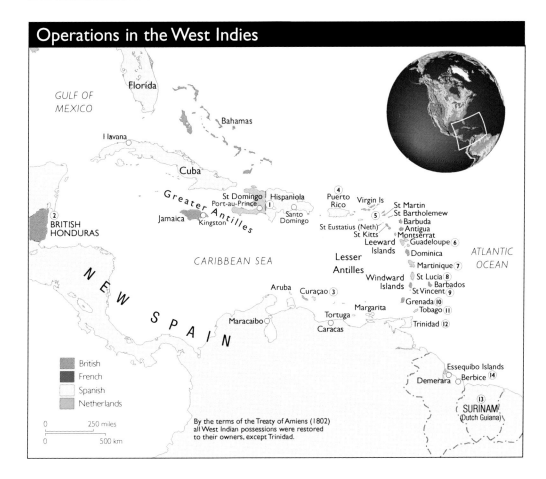

By the terms of the Treaty of Amiens (1802) all West Indian possessions were restored to their owners, except Trinidad.

British
French
Spanish
Netherlands

0   250 miles
0   500 km

1. **St. Domingo/Hispaniola** British attack St. Domingo, 1793; Spanish invade from Hispaniola,1794; Spanish cede Hispaniola to France, 1795; after a long struggle, ex-slaves under native leader L'Ouverture force out British and French in 1798 and unite island as Haiti,1801.
2. **British Honduras** Failed Spanish attack,1798.
3. **Curaçao** Captured by British,1800.
4. **Puerto Rico** Failed British attack,1797.
5. **Dutch Possessions** Captured by British, 1801.
6. **Guadeloupe** Captured by British, 1794; recaptured same year by French, with help from former slaves.
7. **Martinique** Captured by British, 1794; French fail to recapture, 1795.
8. **St. Lucia** Captured by British, 1794. French-supported uprising drives British out, 1795; retaken,1796. **9. St. Vincent** French-supported uprisings drive British out, 1795; retaken, 1796.
10. **Grenada** French-supported uprisings drive British out, 1795; retaken, 1796.
11. **Tobago** Captured by British, 1793.
12. **Trinidad** Captured by British, 1797.
13. **Surinam** Captured by British, 1799.
14. **Demerara, Essequibo and Berbice**. Captured by British, 1796.

the-line, and Admiral Villaret de Joyeuse, with 30 vessels. Villaret managed to protect a vital convoy of grain bound for France from the United States, but lost seven ships and 3,500 seamen in the process; the costly struggle fought over several days culminated on 1 June. After the action the French returned to Brest, tactically defeated, but were nonetheless able to claim a strategic victory since the convoy arrived safely. Britain was able to blockade all French ports, but found it impossible to eradicate all trade, much less to make an impact on the campaigns on land.

In July 1794 a coup brought down Robespierre's government, and with his fall came an end to the Terror and the establishment of a new government known as the Directory. A number of factors explain its rise to power: Robespierre's more moderate Jacobin colleagues began to suspect that they would be the next victims of his

André Masséna. One of Bonaparte's most competent generals, he fought well in Italy in 1794–95 and later distinguished himself in Bonaparte's Italian campaigns of 1796–97, particularly at Montenotte, Dego, Mondovi, Codogno, Lodi and Rivoli. Masséna not only held the Swiss front in 1799 but also drove the Allies back across the Rhine. As C-in-C of the Army of Italy in 1800 he was forced into Genoa, which he surrendered just before Marengo. (Ann Ronan Picture Library)

dictatorship at a time when extreme methods of political control were growing unnecessary; counter-revolutionary movements within France had been crushed; Fleurus had ended the immediate threat to the nation's security; the economic crisis fueled by the weak revolutionary currency, the *assignat*, was abating; and, finally, food was available in greater quantities.

Carnot managed to retain his post at the war ministry; his continued exertions increased the size, morale, and efficiency of the revolutionary armies, just as the allied armies were declining. Moreover, during the autumn, French successes ensured at least temporary security from allied invasion. By August, Jourdan had pushed the Austrians back to the Rhine, while in Holland Pichegru in turn had forced back the Duke of York past Nijmegen. By the beginning of 1795, Holland fell to French control and Pichegru had even managed to capture the Dutch fleet in port. In a bizarre and unique feat in

military history, cavalry crossed the frozen Texel and took possession of the ice-bound ships on 30 January 1795.

The results of the campaign on this front were far-reaching. By the opening months of 1795, France had control of Belgium, Holland, and the left bank of the Rhine, leaving the Allies with nothing but the fortresses of Luxembourg and Mainz. Holland became a satellite friendly to France, known as the Batavian Republic. For the first time during the Revolutionary Wars France could consider invading England, a threat which would naturally cause considerable concern in London and divert important British military and naval resources away from offensive operations and into home defense over the next 10 years.

During the spring of 1795, after a French invasion across the Pyrenees and after numerous failures on other fronts, the alliance began to crumble. Tuscany withdrew her unofficial support for the coalition and Prussia pondered formal withdrawal. At the negotiations held at Basle, Prussian diplomats were left in no doubt of French determination to carry on the war. 'Do you wish to wage a perpetual war with Europe?' asked one French delegate. 'We shall trace with a sure hand the natural limits of the Republic. We shall make sure of the rivers which, after watering several of our departments, take their course toward the sea, and limit the countries now subject to our arms.' Prussia signed a separate peace on 5 April, quickly followed by Saxony, Hesse-Cassel, and Hanover. France also concluded treaties with the new Batavian Republic in May and with Spain in July. Far to the east, the third and final partition of Poland took place on 24 October, so demonstrating the true interests of Prussia, Austria, and Russia, and their lack of unified commitment to challenge France. Meanwhile, on the Rhine the autumn campaign had no decisive result while in northern Italy the French General Schérer defeated the Austrians and Piedmontese at Loano in fierce fighting between 23 and 25 November.

Four major naval actions took place in 1795. In the Mediterranean Admiral Hotham fought

French infantry at the opening of the Italian campaign, 1796. The generally poor state of their appearance was not confined to this theater. In Germany one observer noted: 'The greater part of their infantry was without uniforms, shoes, money, and apparently lacking all organization, if one were to judge by appearances alone. But each man had his musket, his cartridge box, and cockade of [their] national colours, and all were brave and energetic.' It rested with Bonaparte to instill these last virtues into his new command.

two inconclusive actions: on 13–14 March in the Gulf of Genoa, and at Hyères on 13 July, against Admiral Martin's fleet based at Toulon. Cornwallis narrowly escaped capture at the hands of a larger French force off Belle Isle on 17 June, while Admiral Bridport captured several enemy vessels in a minor encounter off Île de Groix on the 23rd. Throughout this time the Royal Navy continued to implement its slow but effective strategy, particularly in the Atlantic, Mediterranean, and Caribbean, of preying on the French merchant marine and the Republic's vast force of privateers. Much further afield, in southern Africa, a British expeditionary force of 1,800 soldiers and sailors conveyed by Admiral Elphinstone landed near Cape Town in August and took possession of the Dutch colony there on 14 September.

The new government, the Directory, had in the meantime taken power in Paris on 22 August. Six weeks later Napoleon Bonaparte, now a general, was called to the streets of Paris to protect the government from a pro-monarchy uprising which took place on 5 October. Deploying his cannon, he swept the demonstrators off the streets with his famous 'whiff of grapeshot'. The Republic faced renewed uprisings in the Vendée at the end of the year, but the rebels were finally defeated in November. By the following spring General Hoche had ended virtually all resistance with the same policy of brutal repression as before. The Revolution, it seemed, was here to stay.

The Campaigns of 1796–97

For the campaign of 1796 the Directory replaced Pichegru with General Jean Victor Moreau. In June, he and Jourdan opened offensives on the Rhine. The Austrian Commander-in-Chief, Archduke Charles, stopped Jourdan's drive, but Moreau managed to cross the Austrian rear, forcing Charles to retire across the Danube. This in turn caused the lesser German states of Württemburg and Baden, among others, to defect from the coalition. At Amberg on 24 August and at Würzburg on 3 September, Charles managed to repel Jourdan's new offensive, but Moreau's success at Schliengen on 23 October ended the year's fighting on the Rhine front with no decisive result.

The critical front was not on the Rhine, but in Italy, where in March the ambitious and energetic Bonaparte was appointed Commander-in-Chief of the republican forces there. Having already made a name for himself at Toulon and Paris, the new commander of the Army of Italy was only 26; he was short, stocky, with shoulder-length, lanky hair, and would dress in a simple blue uniform. One observer recalled his forbidding appearance thus:

His gloomy looks made you think of a man you would not like to meet in a forest after dark. His worn uniform looked so pitiful that I could not believe in the beginning that I was talking to a general. But I soon discovered that he was a very intelligent or at least an unusual man … He sometimes talked a lot and became lively … and then sank into sinister silence …

General André Masséna, on first seeing Bonaparte arrive in Italy, found that 'his

short stature and sickly-looking face did not make a favorable impression on us.' Speaking French with the Italian accent he still retained from his Corsican upbringing, Bonaparte clutched a picture of his new and beautiful wife, Josephine, which he showed to everyone.

The young general was not impressed by the motley forces he was sent to command. Ill-fed, ill-clothed, undisciplined, and only about 45,000 strong, they looked more a rabble than an army, but he was determined to fashion them into a fighting force. In an attempt to inspire his men with grand rhetoric he declared: 'Soldiers! You are badly clad and badly fed. The government owes you much and can give you nothing ... I wish to lead you into the most fertile plains in the world. Rich provinces, large towns will be in your power. It is up to you to conquer them.' The odds were at the time very much against them; but neither they nor their opponents knew that this new commander was both a strategist and a tactician of exceptional caliber.

Facing Bonaparte but separated from one another by a considerable distance were 25,000 Piedmontese under Baron Colli and 35,000 Austrians under General Beaulieu. Bonaparte took advantage of this division to

The Battle of Rivoli, 14 January 1797. In one of his greatest victories of the Revolutionary Wars, Bonaparte not only foiled Alvintzi's attempts to envelop his flanks, but he boldly counterattacked, driving the Austrians from the field and relentlessly pursuing them. Three days later Bonaparte announced that 'The Emperor's fifth army has been entirely destroyed. We have taken 23,000 prisoners...Their flags were embroidered by the hands of the Empress.' (Print after H.E.F. Philippoteaux, Ann Ronan Picture Library)

confront each in turn before the Allies could concentrate. Moving north, he struck the Austrian right flank at Montenotte on 12 April, inflicting 2,500 casualties and thus separating them and the Piedmontese even further. A few days later Bonaparte followed up his success by attacking again, this time driving the Austrians out of Dego with the loss of 4,000 prisoners. The Austrians retook it the next day but then Bonaparte ousted them yet again, forcing Beaulieu to retire on Acqui, to the northeast. Now it was the turn of the Piedmontese, whom Bonaparte confronted at Mondovi on 21 April. After attempting to hold back determined French assaults, Colli's men were finally ejected from the town, with the French close on their heels. Two days later Colli agreed to an armistice and by 28 April Piedmont had effectively been knocked out of the war.

Bonaparte now proceeded towards the Po, which he crossed at Piacenza on 7–8 May, taking the Austrians by surprise and threatening their line of communications with the great fortress-city of Mantua. Leaving Milan and Pavia behind him as he retreated eastwards, Beaulieu fought an epic action at Lodi, where his rearguard attempted to stop the French from crossing a bridge over the Adda. Bonaparte personally led a bayonet assault across the bridge, driving off the defenders and in the process making himself a hero among the French rank and file. With the Austrians retreating towards the Tyrol, Bonaparte made a triumphal entry into Milan on 15 May. He accepted the Austrian surrender of the citadel itself at the end of June. On 21 May Piedmont concluded a peace with France, by which the latter received Nice and Savoy and the right to occupy Piedmont's fortresses. Bonaparte's achievements thus far were nothing short of magnificent: in under three weeks he had bested two armies in turn and had ejected the Austrians from all of Lombardy, with the exception of Mantua. To his soldiers he issued yet another of his epic proclamations:

Soldiers, in fifteen days you have gained six victories, taken twenty-one flags, fifty-five cannon and several strongholds ... You have won battles without cannons, crossed rivers without bridges, you have made forced marches without shoes, bivouacked without brandy and often without bread. Only soldiers of liberty were capable of undergoing all that you have undergone.

And for Bonaparte personally, the victory at Lodi boosted his self-confidence and convinced him that he was set on the road to glory. After Lodi, he would remark later during his exile on St Helena, 'the first spark of high ambition was kindled.'

But there was still much to do. On 30 May Bonaparte crossed the Mincio River with 28,000 men and penetrated Beaulieu's defenses, manned by 19,000 men, at Borghetto. Beaulieu retreated in haste across the Adige, making for the Tyrol, leaving only

Mantua, with its garrison of 13,000 Austrians, free of French control. Bonaparte duly invested the place on 4 June, while new Habsburg forces were rapidly being rushed to the theater of operations from the Tyrol. Under General Quasdanovich came 18,000 troops making for French communications around Brescia. General Würmser, meanwhile, was moving through the valley of the Adige with 24,000 men, in order to relieve Mantua, and a further 5,000 troops were advancing through the Brenta Valley.

Bonaparte had to act quickly and decisively. He withdrew his troops from the siege operations against Mantua and concentrated all available forces, about 47,000 in total, against Quasdanovich near Lake Garda. This left Würmser free to reinforce Mantua, but Bonaparte was making a calculated risk: he could always resume the siege later once his opponents in the field had been vanquished. Quasdanovich foolishly divided his forces into three columns and before he could join forces with Würmser, Bonaparte struck at Lonato on 3 August, capturing one and defeating the other two columns in detail. Now free to take on Würmser, Bonaparte employed his whole force at Castiglione on 5 August, assaulting both Austrian flanks and their rear in a magnificent victory which forced Würmser to retreat across the Mincio and make for the safety of the Tyrol. Once again Bonaparte had employed a masterful strategy, first interposing himself between separate enemy contingents before concentrating against, and defeating, each in turn.

Resuming his siege of Mantua and moving on Trent, Bonaparte caught up with Würmser after a series of forced marches in which French troops covered 30 miles (50 km) in under two days. At Bassano, on 8 September, Bonaparte assailed both enemy flanks and captured an entire Austrian division before Würmser managed to extricate himself. On reaching Mantua with the remnants of his force, Würmser penetrated the siege lines and entered the beleaguered city, bringing the garrison up to 28,000. The Austrians now sought to relieve the city for the third time, sending General Davidovich with 16,000 men down the Adige, while General Alvintzi, with 27,000 men, proceeded with a plan of joining Davidovich at Verona. Detaching forces to keep Davidovich in check, Bonaparte sent 18,000 men against Alvintzi's advance guard at Caldiero on 12 November. While the French withdrew in the face of superior numbers, their determination made Alvintzi think twice about proceeding toward Mantua.

Bonaparte continued to hammer relentlessly at the Austrians, striking again only three days later. Having gone around Alvintzi to the south, he crossed the Adige, turned north and attacked at Arcola on the 15th, attempting a repeat of his previous feat at Lodi by leading his infantry across the bridge over the Alpone. Yet he did not succeed: repeated assaults were repulsed with heavy losses. On the third day of the battle, however, a combination of factors finally brought him victory. Augereau effected a crossing over a trestle bridge, Masséna again attacked across the main bridge, while at the same time behind the Austrian rear a small force of French cavalry blew trumpets and feigned an attack. Alarmed at the possibility of enemy encirclement, the Austrians fled and the wearied French yet again carried the day; this was largely to the credit of Bonaparte's able subordinates.

The year's campaigning had taken a heavy toll on both sides. During the winter of 1796–97 the French and Austrians conducted negotiations for peace. The French suffered from a lack of resources while the Austrians chafed at continued setbacks in the field. These talks ultimately failed, largely because Austria believed that she could still achieve success with yet another offensive in northern Italy. It ended in complete disaster. At the two-day Battle of Rivoli on 14–15 January 1797, the French, whose forces fluctuated in size between 10,000 and 20,000 men, won a decisive victory against about equal numbers. The French took about 11,000 prisoners and inflicted 3,000 casualties at the cost of about 5,000 of their own. In the aftermath of Rivoli, Mantua, desperately clinging on against a determined French siege, now stood as

Austria's last bastion of defense of her Italian possessions. With his supplies reaching a critical stage, Würmser offered to negotiate conditions for surrender. The victor, however, was in no mood to offer terms and brushed aside an envoy's claims that Würmser was still well supplied and prepared to hold out if necessary. On 1 February Bonaparte scoffed at the charade: 'If he [Würmser] had only a fortnight's provisions and spoke of surrendering, he would not deserve an honorable capitulation. Since he sends you, it is because he is reduced to extremity ... If he delays a fortnight, a month, two months, he will still have the same conditions ...' The city surrendered the following day.

French victory at Rivoli, the surrender of Mantua, and the subsequent invasion of Austria itself left the Habsburgs unable to offer further resistance. Bonaparte wrote to the Austrian Commander-in-Chief, Archduke Charles, hoping to provide him with an honorable means of coming to terms: 'Has this war not lasted six years? Have we not killed men enough, and inflicted upon humanity woes enough?' On 17 April, at last aware of their hopeless situation, the Habsburgs agreed to preliminary terms of peace at Leoben. The extent of their military impotence was clear; when the Austrians offered to recognize the French Republic, Bonaparte, with the supreme arrogance of the all-conquering hero, offered a stinging reply: 'The Republic does not require to be recognized, it is the sun at noonday; so much the worse for those who will not see it.'

Exactly six months after agreement was reached at Leoben, more definitive arrangements were made at Campo Formio. The terms were harsher, however, and prompted the Austrians to threaten to renew the fighting. 'Well, the truce is then broken, and the war declared,' Bonaparte replied, 'but remember that before the end of autumn I shall have crushed your monarchy like this porcelain.' The following day, 17 October 1797, the Austrians signed the treaty, whose principal terms required them to acknowledge French control of Belgium and recognize the Cisalpine Republic, a satellite state established in northern Italy constructed from Milan, Modena, the western third of the Venetian Republic, and the northern quarter of the Papal States. In turn, Austria received the Venetian Republic, except for the Ionian Islands, including Corfu, which went to France. Campo Formio did more than see France victorious over the First Coalition; it put France in firm possession of the left bank of the Rhine – a position last achieved nearly 1,000 years before under the reigns of Charlemagne and his immediate successors.

If France was victorious on land, at least for the moment her plans to invade Britain had been frustrated when a Spanish fleet, bound for Brest in order to unite with the French, was discovered and engaged by Admiral Jervis off Cape St Vincent on 14 February 1797. With only 15 ships to the Spaniards' 27, Jervis sailed between the two enemy divisions before closing for the attack. Nelson, perceiving that the Spanish would otherwise unite their forces before Jervis's maneuvers could stop them, broke from the line and blocked the progress of the Spanish

Battle of St Vincent, 14 February 1797. Although the Spanish, with 27 ships-of-the-line carrying 2,308 guns, heavily outnumbered the British, with 15 ships carrying 1,232 guns, the crews of the former were largely landsmen and soldiers with little or no training in seamanship or gunnery. Jervis's victory, which included the capture of four vessels, was almost inevitable, yet it might have been far more complete had he pursued four other vessels disabled in the fight. (Ann Ronan Picture Library)

van, in the process of which his ship became entangled with the rigging of the 80-gun *San Nicolas*. Seizing the moment, Nelson boarded and took her; he then used her deck to board the 112-gun *San Josef*, which stood alongside. He related the final result after the battle:

> ... it was not long before I was on the quarter-deck, when the Spanish captain, with a bended knee, presented me his sword, and told me the admiral was dying with his wounds below. I gave him my hand, and desired him to call to his officers and ship's company that the ship had surrendered, which he did; and on the quarterdeck of a Spanish first-rate, extravagant as the story may seem, did I receive the swords of the vanquished Spaniards ...

All was not well in the Royal Navy, however, for between April and June serious mutinies occurred aboard the fleets at Spithead and the Nore, largely the result of discontentment over bad food, low pay, infrequent leave, and the cruel conduct of some of the captains. The mutiny at Spithead ended on 15 May with the friendly intervention of Lord Howe and Parliament's rapid passage of a new bill promising reforms. The mutiny at the Nore, which occurred on 12 May and ended on 15 June, was more violent and revolutionary in nature. Yet once the government discovered that the ringleader did not enjoy the total support of the crews, it offered a pardon to most of the men, fatally undermining the leadership behind the

Nelson, sword in hand, boarding the *San Josef* at the Battle of Cape St. Vincent. A good impression of the sort of fierce close-quarter fighting which ensued when rival crews met face-to-face. Amongst the British party may be seen soldiers of the 69th Foot, whom Nelson praised for the 'alacrity which will ever do them credit …' (Painting by George Jones, National Maritime Museum)

rebellion. A large number of arrests and more than two dozen executions followed.

The War of the Second Coalition, 1798–1802

The Campaigns in Egypt and Syria, 1798–1801

The collapse of the First Coalition did not affect the ongoing Anglo-French conflict, which continued to be fought at sea and in the West Indies. Fighting was not restricted to the high seas for long, for with the invasion of Britain postponed indefinitely, France now looked elsewhere to strike at her ancient foe. She looked very far afield, indeed: Egypt. Egypt was a self-governing province of the Ottoman Empire, with whom France was at peace, but its annexation could offer an overland route to

India, Britain's most valuable colony. The conquest of Egypt would not only add additional laurels to those won by Bonaparte in Italy, but also would offer potential wealth to France by way of trade.

On 19 May 1798 the Army of Egypt sailed from Toulon, encouraged in Bonaparte's customary fashion: 'Soldiers! The eyes of Europe are upon you. You have great destinies to fulfil … you will do more than you have yet done for the prosperity of your

OPPOSITE Campo Formio marked nothing less than a radical shift in the European balance of power. After only five years of fighting France now received formal Hapsburg recognition of her annexation of Belgium, as well as of her control over the left bank of the Rhine. Since 1792 France had also conquered Holland and northern Italy, thus establishing her 'natural' frontiers: the Rhine, the Pyrenees and the Alps. A myriad of client and dependent states served as buffer zones, which included Switzerland. If Campo Formio owed much to the military successes of the early revolutionary armies, it owed much more to Bonaparte's achievements during the campaigns of 1796–97. These not only established his military reputation, but signaled the period of his political rise, for by 1797 he had forced his government to grant him the power to conclude treaties. Major geographical changes since 1792 were not confined to the west: in the east, Poland had vanished with the partitions of 1793 and 1795.

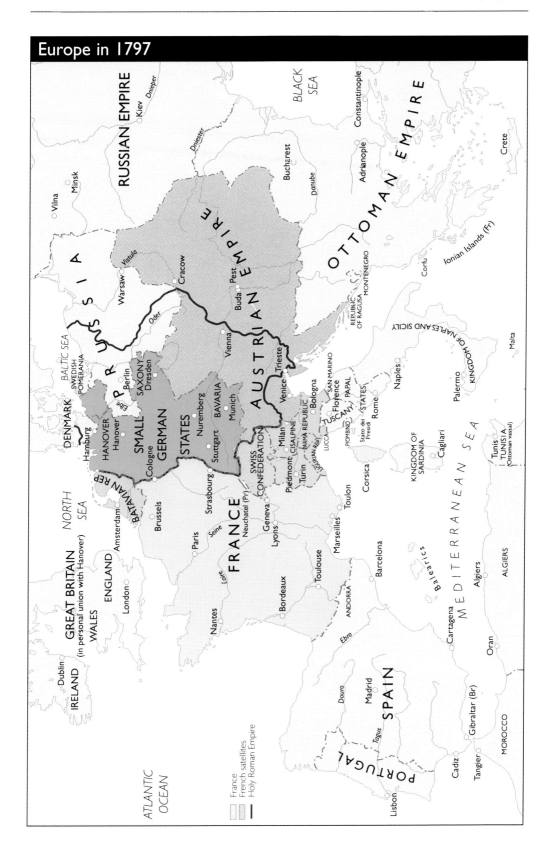

Europe in 1797

ATLANTIC OCEAN

NORTH SEA

GREAT BRITAIN (in personal union with Hanover)

IRELAND
Dublin

WALES

ENGLAND
London

Amsterdam

Paris
Seine
Loire

Nantes

Bordeaux

Toulouse

FRANCE

Lyons

Geneva

Marseilles

Toulon

Barcelona

Balearics

MEDITERRANEAN SEA

ALGIERS

Algiers

ANDORRA
Ebro

SPAIN
Madrid
Douro

PORTUGAL
Tagus

Lisbon

Cadiz

Tangier

MOROCCO

Oran

Cartagena

Gibraltar (Br)

BALTIC SEA

DENMARK

SWEDISH POMERANIA

Hamburg

HANOVER
Hanover

Cologne

BATAVIAN REP

Brussels

Strasbourg

Neuchatel (Pr)

SWISS CONFEDERATION

Elbe

Berlin

SAXONY
Dresden

SMALL GERMAN STATES

Nuremberg

Stuttgart

BAVARIA
Munich

Piedmont
Turin

Milan
CISALPINE

LIGURIAN REP

PARMA REPUBLIC

LUCCA

PIOMBINO

TUSCANY
Florence

Stato dei Presidi

PAPAL STATES

SAN MARINO

Bologna

Rome

Venice

Trieste

AUSTRIAN EMPIRE

Vienna

Buda Pest

Cracow

Oder

Warsaw
Vistula

PRUSSIA

Minsk

Vilna

RUSSIAN EMPIRE

Kiev
Dnieper

Dniester

BLACK SEA

Constantinople

Bucharest

Danube

Adrianople

OTTOMAN EMPIRE

Crete

Ionian Islands (Fr)

Corfu

REPUBLIC OF RAGUSA
MONTENEGRO

KINGDOM OF NAPLES AND SICILY

Naples

Palermo

Malta

Tunis
TUNISIA (Ottoman vassal)

TYRRHENIAN SEA

Cagliari

KINGDOM OF SARDINIA

Corsica

France
French satellites
Holy Roman Empire

Bonaparte in Egypt, 1798. In characteristic style he proclaimed himself the liberator of the oppressed. 'Peoples of Egypt,' he declared, 'you will be told that I have come to destroy your religion; do not believe it! Answer that I have come to restore your rights and punish the usurpers, and that, more than the Mamelukes, I respect God, his Prophet and the Koran.' (Engraving after the painting by Gros, Anne S. K. Brown Military Collection, Brown University Library)

country, the welfare of mankind and your own glory.' The fleet carried 35,000 men aboard 400 transports, escorted by four frigates and 13 ships-of-the-line commanded by Admiral Brueys. The expedition also included a contingent of scientists, artists, and writers who were to study the country's topography, relics, geography, and history. Difficulties quickly arose. 'Even for officers and civilians, things were becoming a little rough,' Baron Denon wrote, recalling conditions aboard the fleet. 'There was hardly any livestock left to supply their table with fresh meat. There was no more fuel to heat our fetid water. The useful animals were disappearing while those which were eating us multiplied a hundred-fold.'

With France and Turkey at peace and the destination of the expedition a secret, the

Ottoman Empire was in no position to defend a possession which, in any event, was scarcely under its own control. A force from the Royal Navy was sent to intercept the French. The First Lord of the Admiralty wrote to Admiral Jervis, the victor of Cape St Vincent, explaining the importance of appointing the right man to command the force:

When you are apprized that the appearance of a British Squadron in the Mediterranean is a condition on which the fate of Europe may at this moment be stated to depend, you will not be surprised that we are disposed to strain every nerve, and incur considerable hazard in effecting it.

The task was entrusted to Vice-Admiral Horatio Nelson who, beginning in May, cruised the Mediterranean with 14 ships-of-the-line and seven frigates in search of the Toulon fleet and Bonaparte's army. In the meantime, on 12 June French forces took possession of Malta, which was ruled by the Knights of St John, an ancient order dating back to the Crusades.

Having successfully eluded Nelson's fleet, and with Malta secure behind him, Bonaparte landed near Marabout on 1 July. He immediately seized Alexandria and advanced on Cairo by land and river. The heat began to take its toll and on reaching the Nile the soldiers made a wild dash for it and flung themselves in, sometimes fully dressed and equipped. Some bathed for hours and many others, so desperate to quench their thirst, drank so much water that they died in the process. 'The soldiers are accusing the generals of the incredible sufferings through which they have gone ever since they left the ships,' one soldier recalled. 'They are crying, they keep asking what wrongs they have done to be sent into the desert to perish in this way.'

The 25,000 French met serious opposition on 21 July in the shape of 21,000 Mamelukes and Turkish infantry who materialized out of the desert and engaged them in a clash of modern versus ancient warriors known as the Battle of the Pyramids. A mass of exotically dressed horsemen faced the great squares of French infantry, deployed in a mutually supporting checkered formation. Desvernois remembered the scene in all its splendor:

... before us were the beautiful Arabian horses, richly harnessed, neighing, snorting, prancing ... their martial riders covered with splendid arms, inlaid with precious metals and stones. They wore very colourful costumes, egret feathers on the turbans, some wore gilded helmets. They were armed with spears, sabres, lances, battle axes and daggers and each wore three pairs of pistols. Their sight, in its novelty and richness, left a vivid impression on our soldiers. From now on, their thoughts dwelt on booty.

The great tide of horsemen charged repeatedly, only to be shot down by disciplined volleys just as they reached the waiting French infantry. 'The number of bodies around our square grew rapidly,' remembered Vertray, 'the clothes of the wounded and dead Mamelukes burnt like tinder.' After losing a quarter of their force, the Mamelukes rode off, unable to stop Bonaparte's inexorable advance.

The following day the French entered Cairo, but they had hardly settled in when Nelson arrived in Aboukir Bay on 1 August and discovered the French fleet lying at anchor. Nelson soon realized that he could maneuver some of his ships to the landward side of the French vessels, whose decks were crowded with stocks of supplies in the expectation that any attack would be confined to seaward. Action began in the late afternoon with an attack on Bruey's van and center, which was slowly pulverized by converging fire. By early evening Bruey had already received two wounds and at about 8 pm, while leaving the poop for the quarter deck, was struck again. The round shot nearly cut him in two, but he refused to be taken below, exclaiming that a French admiral must die on his quarter deck. He was not the only French officer to die heroically. The captain of the *Tonnant*, Dupetit Thouars, had both legs and an arm shot off. He ordered his men to place him in a tub of

The French flagship *L'Orient*, explodes during the Battle of the Nile. In the age of sail fire posed the greatest threat to vessels constructed principally of wood, rope and canvas and carrying large amounts of gunpowder. Nevertheless, ships were remarkably resilient and destruction by conflagration or explosion was unusual, as was sinking. Vessels stricken by excessive damage to hull or rigging or by losses to their crews usually limped away or surrendered. (Painting by George Arnald, National Maritime Museum)

bran, from which he continued to command his ship until he died.

Around 9 pm, well after sunset, a fire broke out aboard the French flagship, *L'Orient*, which soon spread out of control before finally reaching the magazine. Captain Berry, commanding the *Vanguard*, watched the inevitable result with wonder:

The cannonading was partially kept up to leeward of the centre till about ten o'clock, when L'Orient *blew up with a most tremendous explosion. An awful pause and deathlike silence for about three minutes ensued, when the wreck of the masts, yards, etc. which had been carried to a vast height, fell down into the water, and on board the surrounding ships.*

The battle had far-reaching effects. By the early hours of the following morning the French fleet had been annihilated.

The Battle of the Pyramids, 21 July 1798. Bonaparte and his staff, together with dragoons and supply-laden camels, take shelter inside a divisional square. Note the 'colours' or flags borne by the various 'demi-brigades' or regiments. Although flags and standards often identified an army's respective units by the addition of painted or embroidered devices, their principal purpose was to instil *ésprit de corps* and bolster morale. (Painting by General Lejeune, Ann Ronan Picture Library)

Bonaparte's army was left stranded in Egypt without a regular source of supplies or reinforcements from Europe. The Royal Navy had re-established its presence in the Mediterranean. More importantly, Nelson's victory contributed to the formation of a new, second coalition by encouraging the participation of Russia, who viewed the French occupation of Malta and Egypt as a threat to her naval and commercial interests in the Mediterranean.

Seeking further glory and hoping to bring the Ottoman government to terms, Bonaparte meanwhile planned to shift operations to Syria. His campaign was postponed by an uprising in Cairo, and the necessity of leaving sufficient troops in Egypt to maintain order, together with dwindling numbers through disease, left him only 13,000 men and 52 guns with which to conduct the new campaign. The advance began on 10 February 1799. Moving along the coast, he took El Arish on the 19th and Gaza, in the then Turkish province of Syria, about a fortnight later. Yet even greater resistance was offered by the Turks at Jaffa, where they put up a spirited fight for three days before capitulating on 7 March, leaving 2,500 Ottoman prisoners in French hands. Nearly half of these were found to be on

The Battle of the Nile

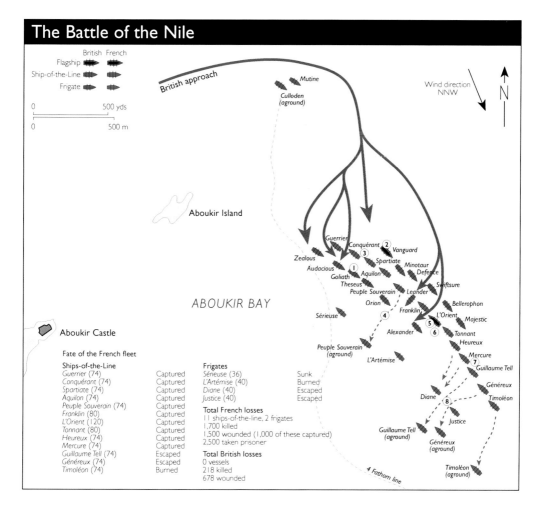

	British	French
Flagship	➤	➤
Ship-of-the-Line	➤	➤
Frigate	➤	➤

0 —————— 500 yds

0 —————— 500 m

British approach

Mutine

Culloden (aground)

Wind direction NNW

N

Aboukir Island

Aboukir Castle

ABOUKIR BAY

Guerrier
Conquérant **2** Vanguard
3
Zealous   Spartiate
Audacious   **1**   Minotaur
Goliath   Aquilon   Defence
Theseus
Peuple Souverain   Leander   Swiftsure
Orion   Bellerophon
Sérieuse   **4**   Franklin   L'Orient   Majestic
Alexander   **5**   Tonnant
6   Heureux
Peuple Souverain (aground)   Mercure
L'Artémise   **7**   Guillaume Tell

Généreux
Diane   **8**   Timoléon
Justice
Guillaume Tell (aground)   Généreux (aground)
Timoléon (aground)

4 Fathom line

Fate of the French fleet

Ships-of-the-Line	
Guerrier (74)	Captured
Conquérant (74)	Captured
Spartiate (74)	Captured
Aquilon (74)	Captured
Peuple Souverain (74)	Captured
Franklin (80)	Captured
L'Orient (120)	Captured
Tonnant (80)	Captured
Heureux (74)	Captured
Mercure (74)	Captured
Guillaume Tell (74)	Escaped
Généreux (74)	Escaped
Timoléon (74)	Burned

Frigates	
Sérieuse (36)	Sunk
L'Artémise (40)	Burned
Diane (40)	Escaped
Justice (40)	Escaped

Total French losses
11 ships-of-the-line, 2 frigates
1,700 killed
1,500 wounded (1,000 of these captured)
2,500 taken prisoner

Total British losses
0 vessels
218 killed
678 wounded

The French fleet lay anchored in Aboukir Bay.

1. 6.30: *Goliath* passes lead French vessel and anchors opposite *Conquérant*; other vessels follow on landward side, including *Audacious*, which pierces the line.

2. Nelson, aboard *Vanguard*, together with other ships, engages French to seaward; all British ships anchor and fighting commences.

3. 6.45: Sunset; leading five ships of French van struggling against eight British vessels; French center resists more steadily, but rear remains unengaged.

4. 9.30: *Peuple Sovereign* drifts off, crippled; *Leander* replaces her to rake *Franklin* and *L'Orient*.

5. 10.00: *L'Orient*, ablaze since 8.00, explodes.

6. 11.15: *Franklin* and, after 12.00, *Tonnant*, surrender; van out of action by midnight.

7. Before dawn: ships of French rear cut their cables and drift south; British ships opposite French van follow in order to engage fresh opponents.

8. Firing continues through the night until about 6 am; surviving French vessels run themselves aground.

Mamelukes and a Bedouin foot soldier. The Mamelukes were a fearless and fearsome élite cavalry force dating back to the 13th century. Heavily armed with pistols, carbine and lance, a warrior galloped at the enemy with his reigns in his teeth, discharged his firearms and threw his lance before finally slashing with his scimitar. Although brilliant horsemen, the Mamelukes possessed no understanding of modern cavalry tactics apart from the charge. (Engraving by Walsh, National Army Museum)

parole, having been previously captured in Egypt. Bonaparte reacted swiftly and ruthlessly. Unable to support these prisoners in the midst of a campaign beset by plague, lack of supplies, and exhaustion, and angered by Turkish violations of the rules of war, he summarily ordered their execution.

Having left behind hundreds of his sick troops in Jaffa, where the plague had devastated the garrison, Bonaparte pushed on for Acre, nearly 160 miles (250 km) further north. Meanwhile, the sick lists mounted. 'The eye disease is truly a horrible plague,' complained Desaix. 'It has deprived me of 1,400 men. In my last marches, I have dragged with me about a hundred of these wretches who were totally blind.' At last, in mid-March, they reached the city and laid siege to the place, easily seeing off at Mount Tabor on 16 April an Ottoman army that had been sent to the relief of Acre. The siege became a costly failure and Bonaparte could go no further. When intelligence reached him that a Turkish force, under British naval escort, was destined from Rhodes to Egypt, he raised the siege and began the long, hard retreat back to Cairo with only about

7,000 men – half his original force. Bourrienne recalled this ghastly affair: 'I saw with my own eyes officers who had limbs amputated being thrown out of their litters [by their attendants] ... amputated men, wounded men, plague-stricken men, being abandoned in the fields.'

When Bonaparte finally reached Cairo in early June he found 20,000 Turks under Mustafa Pasha waiting to disembark from British ships. Rather than marching on the capital Mustafa took the fortress at Aboukir on 15 July and prepared defensive works in expectation of French attack. Bonaparte duly appeared 10 days later and, defeating the Turks on open ground, accepted the surrender of the fortress on 2 August.

While negotiating the release of Turkish prisoners into British protection, Bonaparte learned of the first French defeats on the Continent at the hands of the forces of the Second Coalition. It was time to return home. Immediately abandoning the Army of Egypt to its fate under Kléber, he made for France by frigate on 24 August. He eluded Royal Navy patrols and landed at Fréjus on 9 October, hailed as a victor, his reputation not only intact but enhanced.

Kléber had been ordered to continue the occupation and resist Turkish and British

General Abercromby, wounded at Alexandria, 21 March 1801. Having landed at Aboukir Bay a fortnight earlier in the face of determined French resistance, Abercromby advanced on Alexandria where he was attacked by Menou on the night of the 20th–21st. After confused and savage fighting lasting until dawn the French withdrew, having suffered 3,000 casualties to the British 1,400. Abercromby died a few days later of a gunshot wound to his thigh. (Ann Ronan Picture Library)

efforts to dislodge him, but he recognized his vulnerability and soon opened negotiations. He received generous terms: by the Convention of El Arish, agreed on 21 January 1800, the Turks granted him leave to evacuate his troops back to France on British warships. But Kléber was to be bitterly disappointed: Admiral Sir Sidney Smith, who had signed the agreement, had had no authorization from the British government to conclude such terms, and when London refused to ratify the convention Kléber went on the offensive in the hopes of improving his negotiating position. On 20 March, he defeated the Turks at Heliopolis, thus preserving Cairo in French hands, but this did not alter the unpleasant fact that he and his dwindling army still remained marooned in Egypt.

It was, however, to be Kléber's last success, for a religious fanatic assassinated him with a

Turkish infantry and cavalry. Ottoman forces which opposed the French were generally of dubious quality and proved no match against a modern, well-disciplined European force. The Janissaries, originally composed of boys drawn from the Ottoman provinces in the Balkans, were exceptional, having been specially trained to fight since childhood. Turkish troops were raised by local *pashas* who had to meet specific quotas and arm and equip their men at personal expense. (Engraving by Walsh, Ann Ronan Picture Library)

1. **France** Technically speaking, the new coalition began with the Anglo-Russian alliance in December 1798, but France was still at war with Britain and had already opened hostilities with Turkey by invading Egypt in June.
2. **Britain** Against France since February 1793.
3. **Austria** Against France, June 1799–February 1801.
4. **Russia** Against France, December 1798–1801; troops withdrawn, 1799.
5. **Ottoman Empire** June 1798–1802.
6. **Batavian Republic** French ally since 1795.
7. **Naples** Against France November 1798–March 1801.
8. **Spain** French ally since 1796. Invaded Portugal, 1801.
9. **Portugal** Against France since 1793 until 1801.
10. **Small German states of the Holy Roman Empire** Nearly all neutral, except Bavaria, acting under pressure from Austria, 1799–1801 and briefly Wurttemberg and Hesse-Darmstadt.
11. **Northern and Central Italian States** All French puppet regimes except neutral Parma and hostile Tuscany.
12. **Malta** Opposed French occupation, June 1798–September 1800.
13. **Switzerland** French puppet state from 1798.

Archduke Charles of Austria. Brother of the Emperor Francis, he contributed to victory at Neerwinden but later failed at Wattignies and Fleurus. He nevertheless possessed a sound grasp of tactics and organization and won victories during the Rhine campaign in 1796. During operations in Italy in 1797 he managed to save his army where other Austrian commanders failed, making him the only senior general to retain a respectable reputation at war's end. In 1799, he stopped the French offensive over the Rhine and pushed Masséna back from Zürich during operations in Switzerland. (Ann Ronan Picture Library)

knife on 14 June, after which command devolved on General Menou, who, alone of the French generals, had converted to the Muslim faith during the campaign. British efforts to drive the French from Egypt were intensified when General Ralph Abercromby, with 15,000 men, made an amphibious landing near Alexandria in March 1801. There, on the 21st, the French were driven back and Abercromby was killed. By the end of August, Menou was obliged to capitulate on remarkably similar terms to those reached at El Arish, with French troops to return home aboard British vessels. Looking back on the campaign, General Marmont summed it up accurately: 'All chances were against, not a single one was in our favour. With a light heart we walked into almost certain doom.

Belligerent powers in the second coalition

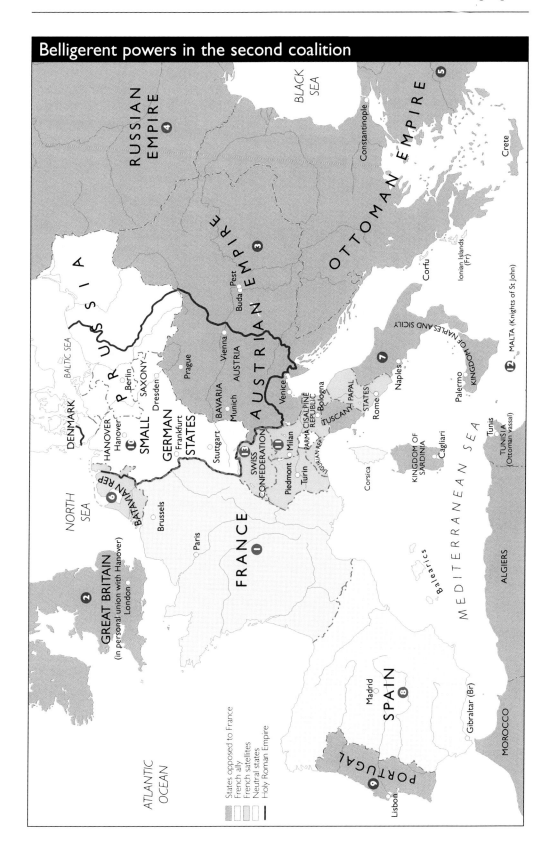

States opposed to France
French ally
French satellites
Neutral states
Holy Roman Empire

ATLANTIC
OCEAN

NORTH
SEA

BALTIC SEA

BLACK
SEA

RUSSIAN EMPIRE ④

OTTOMAN EMPIRE

Constantinople

Crete

Ionian Islands (Fr)

Corfu

P R U S S I A

Berlin

DENMARK

HANOVER
Hanover ①

SMALL
GERMAN
STATES

SAXONY
Dresden

Frankfurt

BAVARIA
Munich

Stuttgart

Prague

Vienna
AUSTRIA

AUSTRIAN EMPIRE ③

Buda
Pest

Venice

BATAVIAN REP ⑥

Brussels

GREAT BRITAIN
(in personal union with Hanover) ②

London

F R A N C E ①

Paris

SWISS
CONFEDERATION ⑬

Piedmont

Turin

Milan
CISALPINE
REPUBLIC ⑪

PARMA

LIGURIAN REP.

Bologna

TUSCANY

PAPAL
STATES

Rome

KINGDOM OF NAPLES AND SICILY

Naples

Palermo

KINGDOM OF
SARDINIA

Cagliari

Corsica

Balearics

S P A I N ⑧

Madrid

Gibraltar (Br)

MOROCCO

ALGIERS

TUNISIA
(Ottoman vassal)

Tunis

MALTA (Knights of St John) ⑫

PORTUGAL ⑨

Lisbon

M E D I T E R R A N E A N   S E A

⑤

⑦

One must admit, it was an insane gamble, and even its success would not have justified it.'

Operations in Europe, 1799–1801

While Bonaparte was occupied in Egypt in 1798, the Great Powers were engaged in diplomatic efforts to raise a new coalition. Austria wanted revenge on the French for the terms of Campo Formio. While Britain was still at war with France there remained a framework around which to build resistance against France once again. The new alliance contained Britain, Russia, Austria, Naples, Portugal, and a host of lesser German states. This was an impressive array of power, but the coalition's plans did not recognize the strategic importance of Switzerland as an avenue of invasion into France, relying instead on separate offensives in unconnected regions including Italy, southern Germany, and Holland.

Field Marshal Alexander Suvorov. Russia's most able senior commander, he achieved victories during the campaign of 1799 at Cassano, the Trebbia, and Novi largely through the use of unimaginative yet determined bayonet attacks, a tactic he had successfully employed in the wars against the Turks. In his book, *How to Win*, Suvorov instructed his men to 'Fire sparingly, but fire accurately. Thrust home forcefully with the bayonet. A bullet can go astray, but the bayonet doesn't.' (Roger-Viollet)

The Directory, like the allied governments, had its own ambitious plans for the coming campaign. These involved offensive operations in Naples under Macdonald, in northern Italy conducted by Schérer, and in Switzerland led by Masséna, and Jourdan, together with Bernadotte, on the east side of the Rhine. General Brune, with 25,000 men, was to defend Holland against expected Anglo-Russian amphibious operations. Every French army was considerably understrength and none possessed the high level of morale so characteristic of the Army of Italy under Bonaparte in 1796–97. Under these adverse circumstances, and with Bonaparte far off in Egypt, France faced a challenge that would prove difficult to overcome.

The campaign opened when French forces attacked and quickly occupied the mainland possessions of the Kingdom of Naples in early 1799, establishing another satellite state known as the Parthenopean Republic. On the main Italian front, Schérer failed to capture Verona before the Austrian troops could unite with the Russians, who were marching west under Field Marshal Alexander Suvorov, a veteran of the various wars fought against Poland and Turkey since the 1760s. In the middle of April General Moreau replaced

Schérer, while at about the same time Suvorov arrived and began a campaign which drove the French toward Genoa and beat another army under Macdonald at the River Trebbia. Along the Rhine, Jourdan got no further than Stockach by the end of March and by the summer fighting focused on Switzerland, with the Austrians led by their able Commander-in-Chief, Archduke Charles. Masséna had by then made initial progress in Switzerland, but he was obliged to give ground when Jourdan was driven back. Nevertheless, in June he was able to stop Charles's advance near Zürich.

In the summer of 1799, the French military situation was bleak. More Russians were headed west and the Allies enjoyed a substantial overall numerical superiority. General Gouvian Saint Cyr, the commander of the French army in Rome, complained that

the greatest enemies … were neither the Austrians, nor the Russians, nor the bands of Piedmontese brigands. It was the scarcity of money, of provisions, of clothing … and often of ammunition. Never had an army been so forsaken by the government, and never had one suffered more privations.

Both August offensives – at Novi in Italy and at Mannheim on the Rhine – failed, and it seemed that at least one allied army would

Flushed with victory, the élite Consular Guard – the forerunners of Napoleon's Imperial Guard – pursue the broken Austrian rearguard at Marengo. 'We drove them down to the bridge over the Bormida, using our sabres all the way,' wrote Eugène de Beauharnais, Bonaparte's stepson, and a captain in the *Chasseurs à cheval*. 'The mêlée lasted for ten minutes and I was lucky to suffer nothing worse than two sabre cuts on my shabraque [saddle blanket].' (Roger-Viollet)

break through into France itself. In short, by the summer of 1799 the Directory had lost most of northern Italy, and with the defeat and death of Joubert at Novi on 15 August all of Bonaparte's gains in 1796–97 had been reversed.

It is ironic that the changes in allied strategy instigated by Austria and implemented in early September saved France from almost certain ruin. The Russian presence near the Rhine and northern Italy began to concern Austria, who wished to restrict her partner's influence in regions where she felt Habsburg interests were paramount. Because Archduke Charles had been shifted from Switzerland to the Rhine, Suvorov and his new reinforcements had no option but to remain near Zürich to face Masséna, who had recently been strengthened by the arrival of his own reinforcements.

Meanwhile, an Austrian army under General Michael Melas was to move against

Marengo, 14 June 1800. Unexpectedly opposed by superior numbers, Bonaparte struggled as Melas enveloped his right flank, pressed his center to the point of collapse and drove the French back for several miles. Convinced that the day was won, Melas then marched off while Bonaparte rallied his men and summoned reinforcements. With morale restored and fresh troops at hand, Bonaparte counterattacked, striking the front of the Austrian advance guard and hitting the flank of the main body, causing a rout. Half the Austrian force became casualties or prisoners. (The Art Archive/Musee de Versailles/Dagli Orti)

Provence from northern Italy, and an Anglo-Russian expedition was preparing to land in North Holland. In late August Suvorov was ordered to threaten Masséna's right flank, but the Russians' problems with supply and the necessity of fighting their way into position gave Masséna time to defeat allied forces for a second time at Zürich on 25–26 September. Finally, in October, the tide turned against the Allies: Switzerland was cleared of Austrian and Russian troops and, after a series of defeats culminating at Bergen, the Anglo-Russian force in North Holland was ignominiously obliged to evacuate.

Severely disappointed by these setbacks and jealous of Britain's capture and occupation of Malta, Tsar Paul left the coalition in December. By this time Bonaparte had arrived back in France and had seized power (the coup of Brumaire) in Paris on 9–10 November, establishing a new government known as the Consulate, with himself as its principal, or First, Consul.

French and Allied diplomats conducted peace negotiations during the winter of 1799–1800, but no agreement was forthcoming and the belligerents prepared to renew fighting in the spring.

Two Austrian armies gave immediate concern to the French. On the Rhine, Field Marshal Paul Kray had 140,000 men; in northern Italy, Melas commanded over 100,000. Bonaparte instituted a host of new army reforms, organizing his forces into corps, levying new troops, and establishing a Reserve Army of 50,000 men, based at Dijon. Although it appears that he intended to carry his army into Germany when the spring campaign season began, this plan depended on the support of Moreau who, as Commander-in-Chief on the Rhine, could march through Switzerland and threaten Kray from the rear. Moreau demurred, however, preferring instead to confront the Austrians in a more orthodox offensive against their front. Bonaparte's revised plan was to strike the Austrians in Italy, beginning at the end of March, but this scheme also had to be shelved when the Austrians, under Melas, opened their own Italian offensive in early April.

Melas's campaign opened successfully until he foolishly halted, thinking that Genoa was about to fall to his forces, instead of proceeding directly into France itself. Grasping this unexpected opportunity, Bonaparte pushed the Reserve Army through the Great St Bernhard Pass and over the Alps.

Bonaparte crossing the Alps, May 1800. Tens of thousands of soldiers of the Army of Reserve braved the bitter cold, snowfall and the risk of avalanche in an attempt to reach Italy before the Austrians could take Genoa. Moving through the Great St Bernard and several other passes, French troops descended into the Lombard plain. On learning of Bonaparte's arrival in Italy, Melas proceeded from Nice and shortly after gave battle at Marengo on 14 June. (Painting by Jacques-Louis David, Roger-Viollet)

It was an effort of epic proportions, reminiscent of Hannibal's exploit 20 centuries before. One senior French officer recalled: 'We were all proceeding along the goat paths, men and horses, one by one. The artillery was dismounted, also the guns, and put into hollowed-out tree trunks which were drawn on ropes ... After we reached the summit, we sat down on the snow and slid downward.' This remarkable achievement enabled Bonaparte to position himself across the enemy rear and the decisive encounter took place at Marengo on 14 June. The day did not begin well for Bonaparte. 'Yes, the battle is lost,' General Desaix declared defiantly, 'but it is only three o'clock. There is still time to win another one.' And indeed there was.

While the Austrians ineptly pursued the retreating French, Bonaparte reorganized his troops. When reinforcements arrived, he launched a determined counterattack against the enemy's disorganized columns. When Kellermann charged with his cavalry against an exposed flank the Austrians disintegrated into a rout, and what might have been a serious French defeat was converted into one of Bonaparte's most famous victories. The cost was, nevertheless, high: the French suffered 7,000 casualties to the Austrians' 6,000, but Bonaparte took 8,000 prisoners and 40 guns.

Two days after Marengo, Bonaparte and Melas arranged a truce with Bonaparte clearly holding the upper hand. 'Sir,' he declared to Melas's envoy,

my conditions are irrevocable ... Your position is as well known to me as to yourself. You are in Alessandria, encumbered with the dead, the wounded and the sick, and destitute of provisions; you have lost the elite of your army. You are surrounded on all sides. I could exact everything, but I only demand of you what the situation of affairs imperatively requires ...

Appreciating their dire situation, the Austrians surrendered all fortresses west of the Mincio and south of the Po, but it was by no means a definitive end to the war. Bonaparte therefore appealed directly to the Emperor Francis:

On the battlefield of Marengo, surrounded by the sufferers and in the midst of 15,000 dead bodies, I implore your Majesty to hear the cry of humanity, and not to allow the offspring of two brave and powerful nations to slaughter one another for the sake of interests of which they know nothing.

The truce held, but Austria refused to rule out further recourse to arms.

British diplomacy now decided the issue. When Pitt extended further subsidies to support Habsburg resistance, hostilities resumed in late November. While Bonaparte remained in Paris in order to manage political matters, he ordered Moreau to move directly on Vienna, supported by Brune along the Adige and Macdonald in the Alps. The final land battle of the Revolutionary Wars was about to be played out.

At sea, Britain faced a new threat from an unlikely source. Angered by Britain's maritime dominance, Tsar Paul, together with Denmark, Sweden, and Prussia, agreed in December 1800 to establish the League of Armed Neutrality. The League would cooperate to prevent British warships from searching or seizing commercial vessels with cargoes the Royal Navy classified as contraband goods. This posed a direct challenge to Britain's Maritime Code and threatened her important Baltic trade. In March 1801, the new government under Henry Addington swiftly dispatched Admiral Sir Hyde Parker, with 26 ships-of-the-line, to the Baltic to negotiate with Denmark and Sweden in the hopes of detaching them from their obligations to the League. The last great naval encounter of the war was soon to be fought by Parker's celebrated second-in-command, the hero of the Nile, Horatio Nelson.

Orthodox Warfare

How did the armies of the French Revolutionary Wars fight and were they different from their predecessors? In simple terms, all European armies, except the French, fought according to carefully established patterns set earlier in the century which they continued to follow in the 1790s. Eighteenth-century armies were the property of their autocratic rulers. They were paid professionals – clothed, disciplined, and trained by the state and as such employed at the discretion of the monarch when and where occasion demanded it. European armies were instruments of royal power: what the king did with his army was his business at a time when the concept of the 'nation' had yet to emerge.

Armies were divided into three arms: infantry, cavalry, and artillery. The bulk of armies consisted of the infantry, which for the whole of the 18th century had fought with smoothbore, flintlock muskets, which could be fitted with a socket bayonet. Thus armed, the foot soldier could, after following a strict sequence of evolutions, deliver one or two rounds a minute while deployed in carefully dressed ranks, three men deep. Linear tactics were the order of the day and little emphasis was placed on complex maneuvers, though infantry were trained to deploy in column and square as circumstances required. Skirmishing and light infantry tactics, which had been developed in the Seven Years' War and the conflicts in North America, became more evident on European battlefields after 1800.

Infantry tactics demanded a high level of training and discipline, as it was no easy matter to maintain control over large bodies of men who were not only expected to deploy from column to line, but to maintain impeccable formation, receive and give fire, and advance with the bayonet. This system not only discouraged individual initiative, it deliberately reduced the infantryman to an automaton whose sole function was to execute the orders of his NCOs and officers without question and with maximum efficiency. Cavalry largely played the role of shock troops, charging with saber or lance against an enemy weakened beforehand by musket and artillery fire. Until the French Revolutionary Wars artillery was used rather unimaginatively; having placed his guns along the line as he saw fit, a commander seldom attempted to maneuver them in the course of the fighting in order to coordinate his efforts with those of the other two arms.

Such armies were excessively expensive to feed, equip, and train, and so commanders were loathe to sacrifice them to the dangers of battle unless absolutely obliged to do so. Saxon military doctrine in the mid-18th century stated this plainly: 'A battle is at once the most important and most dangerous operation of war ... A great general shows his mastery by attaining the object of his campaign by sagacious and sure maneuvers, without incurring any risk.' It is not surprising that 18th-century warfare was thus characterized by its focus on siege operations. Fortresses that surrendered spared both sides the massive casualties that resulted from pitched battles where long lines of infantry blazed away at each other with less than 100 yards between them.

All 18th-century armies relied heavily on their supply trains and fixed magazines. Hundreds of wagons and supply vehicles followed the armies, together with thousands of officers' attendants, camp followers, and other noncombatant service personnel, making the progress of armies slow and cumbersome. Supply and communication depended on securing fortresses and magazines, which in turn limited the geographical scope of operations and dictated the speed at which they could be conducted.

Revolutionary Warfare

The new form of warfare introduced during the 1790s called all of this into question. The fact that the armies of the *ancien régime* failed to adapt to the changes goes far in explaining their consistent failures. What, then, had changed? There were no great technological innovations at this time, so improved weaponry is not the explanation. Apart from limited use of semaphore and the observation balloon, nothing substantially new emerged in this period. First, there was the intangible element of motivation: 'You can hope for victory not just because of the numbers and the discipline of our soldiers;

you will win it only through the progress the republican spirit will make in the armed forces.' So declared the revolutionary leader St Just in February 1793. But was it this spirit that ultimately led to victory? To an extent that is impossible to measure, it was. Motivation cannot, of course, be quantified, but there is no denying that many men went off to the front with the courage of their convictions that the cause of the Revolution was just and honorable and therefore worthy of supreme effort on the battlefield.

Naturally the authorities encouraged this feeling in every way, distributing thousands of propaganda leaflets to the troops, and encouraging them with patriotic speeches about their duty to the people as well as to the nation. Singing and music played a part. Captain Vernay remembered an incident on the eve of the Battle of the Pyramids:

At sunrise, military music suddenly burst upon us. The supreme commander had ordered the Marseillaise to be played, knowing its effect on the soldiers. This marvelous song incites the soldiers' courage, inflames their patriotism and makes them realize that the time for complaints has passed and that their job is to be victorious.

Yet motivation alone cannot explain French success, for although the élan of French troops remained fairly consistent, French armies were defeated from time to time.

Numerical superiority certainly played an essential – and perhaps *the* most essential – role in French success. An examination of the numbers employed by both sides in the great battles of the war, particularly in the crucial early period, reveals that only when the French enjoyed a clear numerical advantage were they victorious. After the introduction of the *levée en masse* in August 1793, French numerical superiority was more or less assured on at least one front and often on others as well. Deficient records make it impossible to determine exactly how large the armies of republican France were, but it is a fact that the *levée en masse* created the largest fighting force ever seen in European history up to that time. For the opening of the decisive campaign of 1794 France probably fielded about 800,000 men –

A *Représentant en Mission* addressing French troops. During the Terror (1793–94), political commissars monitored the loyalty of soldiers at the front and inculcated in them the virtues of the Revolution through music, reading material, and speeches. Wielding absolute power and employing a network of spies, they could order the arrest and even death of anyone they suspected of disloyalty or even sloth. 'I know neither Generals nor special powers,' one declared. 'I alone command here and I shall be obeyed.' (Roger-Viollet)

French artillery in action, 1792. As the artillery contained the smallest proportion of aristocrats in the early years of the Revolution this arm suffered least from the mass exodus and resignation of former royal army officers and men which so weakened the infantry and, to a much greater extent, the cavalry. Indeed, the regular artillery of the old army was responsible for the victory at Valmy and the consequent preservation of revolutionary France. (Print after H. Lecomte, Roger-Viollet)

a truly staggering figure when one compares this to the armies of her opponents, who numbered only slightly over half as many.

Contrary to popular belief, the military doctrines and philosophies that underpinned the new forms of warfare unleashed by the French Revolutionary Wars were not new and cannot, therefore, be called revolutionary. Nevertheless, it was the French who made the best and most imaginative use of these principles and their adversaries were fatally slow to catch on. Even as the French Revolution was altering forever the political face of France – and soon much of Europe – a process of military revolution was already under way. The two movements coincided and it was the French who reaped the benefits, partly from necessity and partly from the fact that so many of these new ideas originated in the minds of French military theorists of the *ancien régime*. This was partly a consequence of the military disasters of the Seven Years'

War, where French martial decline was shockingly exposed for all to see.

The collapse of discipline and consistently poor battlefield performances inspired men such as the Comte de Gribeauval (1715–89) to institute fundamental reforms in several important ways. Gribeauval, an experienced artillery officer, brought significant improvements to this arm of service by standardizing the caliber of field pieces, by introducing the idea of interchangeable parts, and by enhancing the accuracy of fire and improving mobility in the field. The French ultimately became masters of the use of artillery and a great part of their success must be attributed to the influence of Napoleon Bonaparte, who was himself trained as a gunner. Hereafter warfare would never be the same, and over time artillery would gradually hold a formidable place on every European battlefield.

While Gribeauval undertook reform of the artillery arm, the great French foreign minister and later minister for war, Choiseul, persuaded Marshal de Broglie, then commanding forces in Germany in 1759, to adopt new forms of troop formations designed to provide greater speed and mobility. By dividing his army into smaller units, or 'divisions', and by providing each division with its own complement of light infantry acting as a screen for the formed units, Broglie permitted divisional commanders in the field a degree of initiative and flexibility hitherto unknown. At the same time the division rendered columns of troops more manageable and easier to deploy into line on the approach of the enemy. Divisions could also move relatively independently of one another and, being sufficiently numerous in troops of all three arms, were capable of fighting an adversary on its own for a limited time or until another division appeared to assist it.

The French and, above all, Bonaparte, used these new techniques to excellent effect during the Revolutionary Wars, particularly from 1796, when the divisional system was introduced throughout the French army. Although the permanent use of army corps was not introduced until 1804, Moreau was the first to adopt this formation in the campaign of 1800 when, on finding control and administration of the 11 divisions of the Army of the Rhine rather cumbersome, he organized them into four corps.

After Choiseul, Saint German introduced further reforms that raised the standard of professionalism in the officer corps and improved discipline. In the late 1780s, the Comte de Guibert trimmed the army of its enormously inefficient and expensive officer corps, particularly top-heavy with generals. Thus, by the eve of the Revolutionary Wars,

the far-reaching innovations and reforms of the previous generation had become firmly fixed and it only remained for them to be tested in the next contest. When that next contest came in the form of the Revolutionary Wars, the French, unlike their adversaries, introduced radical changes in their leadership. Within the officer corps, the Terror saw to it – by nothing less than the liberal use of the guillotine – that the army was purged of suspected royalists, 'traitors', and those supposedly lacking the will to attack the enemy. Speaking of the generals of 1793, one Convention delegate declared that

the majority of the leaders were, if not ready to betray the Republic, at least but little disposed to make the great sacrifices for that form of government. Few generals had sprung from the ranks of the people, and there was no doubt that a certain number of them regretted [the end of] the constitutional monarchy under which they thought themselves destined to the highest offices ...

Charges were made in an atmosphere of frenzied excitement in Paris and many a loyal and well-meaning general lost his head to the madness that swept the capital in the wake of defeat. On his condemnation as a traitor in July 1793, General Custine could only declare, hopeless yet defiant: 'I have no more defenders; they have disappeared. My conscience charges nothing against me. I die calm and innocent.' It is a chilling fact that more French generals met their deaths by this means than were killed in combat. Whereas 80 generals fell in action during the 1790s, 84 died at the hands of the revolutionaries in 1793–94 alone.

Although the French were the clear leaders in military reform, other armies, including those of Austria, Britain, and Russia, made various reforms of their own in the generation preceding the French Revolutionary Wars. The Austrians had introduced the use of light troops during their mid-century wars with Prussia. The infantry, often dressed in green as a rudimentary form of camouflage, screened the front of infantry columns and sniped at the enemy, often from cover. Light cavalry was used for reconnaissance, raids, and for forays against enemy flanks and supply lines. The British, too, introduced new light infantry formations, such as the 60th Foot, based on their unfortunate experiences in the woods of North America. Later, during the French Revolutionary Wars themselves, Sir John Moore (of later Peninsular War fame), would make great strides in light infantry training. Yet it was the French who made maximum use of such troops, screening their formed bodies with skirmishers to their front – nimble, quick, independently minded soldiers who harassed the enemy with individually aimed fire which enabled friendly columns and lines to advance under at least a limited form of cover. Precisely

French infantry (left) routing Hungarian infantry at Thionville, October 1792. Reliance on the bayonet was a fundamental military precept of the early revolutionary armies. As General Hoche put it, 'no manoeuvring, nothing elaborate, just cold steel, passion and patriotism.' (After H. Lecomte, Roger-Viollet)

at a time when other armies were deploying many fewer light troops – in more linear formations and in more limited roles – the French were expanding both their role and numbers and employing light troops as an integral part of their ordinary line regiments.

Yet it was the French who made maximum use of an existing infantry formation – the column. Soldiers deployed in column were densely packed, ensuring better discipline, more unit cohesion, and better protection from cavalry than when formed in line. Whereas the line consisted of men deployed side by side in companies only three ranks deep, the column generally maintained a front of just one or two companies. The remainder was positioned immediately behind, giving a depth of 12 ranks to a battalion of eight companies with a two-company front. The great Marshal de Saxe, victor of Fontenoy in 1745, had experimented with this formation for use in assault, but it was the French

revolutionaries who brought it into the mainstream of battlefield tactics. The column was the most effective means of harnessing the power of the large numbers of raw recruits that the *levée en masse* produced. Even if there had been time available to train such men to fight in carefully deployed lines, the natural independence of the new 'free' citizen militated against the old methods of strict and often brutal discipline necessary to achieve such precision.

By thus arranging men in depth, revolutionary generals could utilize the shock power of massed infantry as never before. A column could be deployed and maneuvered with greater flexibility than any previously used formation, while at the same time it brought force of numbers to bear against the narrow depth of an enemy line. Columns could march, redeploy for attack, change into line or square and detach skirmishers with relative ease – precisely what was needed in armies composed of untrained conscripts with no experience of firing a musket or marching in step. The independence of skirmishing suited some of the men defending freedom, but for the bulk of them, herded together in great masses that relied on the power of the bayonet, the

attack column was the ideal formation. Many a republican general could attribute at least part of his victory to his reliance on, and regular employment of, this formation.

Thus, over time, the French armies learned to employ flexible tactics according to the terrain and circumstances of the battlefield. While their weapons were no better than their adversaries', they made excellent use of attacking columns – making a virtue of necessity by employing their enormous numbers in the form of great phalanxes of bayonets pushed forward against an enemy whose thin lines consistently broke under the weight of sheer numbers.

Crucially, the French were far less encumbered by the enormous supply trains of their *ancien régime* counterparts. 'The Romans are supposed to have marched twenty-four miles in a day,' Bonaparte proudly observed in 1797. 'Our half-brigades, however, are marching thirty miles, and during the rest

A British baggage-wagon, bearing not only the personal effects of the soldiers, but their wives and children as well. Such vehicles and noncombatants considerably encumbered allied armies on the march, giving the French, who traveled lighter and depended more heavily on the land, a distinct advantage in mobility. (Print after W. H. Pyne)

periods they fight.' While the armies of the Allies trundled along, their movements severely restricted by dependence on their vast columns of supply wagons, the French relied on the resources around them. As Carl von Clauswitz, the great military theorist, would later observe in his classic work *On War*:

The French Revolutionary leaders cared little for depots and even less for devising a complicated mechanism that would keep all sections of the transport system running like clockwork. They sent their soldiers into the field and drove their generals into battle – feeding, reinforcing and stimulating their armies by having them procure, steal, and loot everything they needed.

Often troops were billeted on the local population, who had no choice but to feed them. Bonaparte in particular devoted a great deal of attention to logistical planning, supplementing the practice of living off the land by providing adequate stocks of food and supplies at advanced depots.

Finally, Bonaparte brought not only dash and charisma to his leadership qualities, but also a firm grasp of simple strategic principles. 'With few exceptions, the most numerous

French light cavalry in action. These troopers carried a curved saber used for slashing while their heavier counterparts wielded a straight, broader sword used for thrusting. With a few exceptions French cavalry during the Revolutionary Wars performed indifferently, but would come into its own under the Empire (1804–14). (Edimedia)

army can be sure of victory,' he observed in 1797. 'Therefore, the art of war consists of being superior wherever you want to attack. If your army is smaller than that of your enemy, do not allow him the time to unite his forces.' He understood that victory lay in striking one's opponent at its critically weak point with superior forces. If that meant drawing forces away from other objectives, so be it. The victorious commander could return to secondary tasks having first confronted and beaten the enemy's main army.

Weapons, Equipment, and Uniforms

Soldiers of the 18th century were elaborately uniformed and equipped, making battle not simply a contest of arms, but an impressive spectacle of color and sartorial extravagance. At the start of the wars the French armies

Austrian infantryman in the uniform worn during the War of the First Coalition. German regiments wore white tunics with collars and cuffs of distinguishing regimental colors. Hungarian units wore the same tunic but with distinctive sky-blue trousers. Note also the canteen and short sword worn on the left hip and ammunition pouch on the right. (Print after R. von Ottenfeld)

wore a mixture of styles: the old regular units continued to wear the white of the *ancien régime* with colored facings and an old-fashioned helmet; newly raised units wore the dark blue of the *Garde National* and the bicorn hat. In 1793, all French infantry began to wear blue coats with red facings and white lapels, though shortage of supplies prevented total uniformity. To describe the varied appearances of the armies of this period is impossible, but, like France, most European armies had long since adopted a basic color scheme to clothe their infantry, with some variations in the cavalry and artillery: scarlet for Britain; white for Austria; dark green for Russia; and dark blue for Prussia.

Brightly colored uniforms would appear on the face of it entirely ill-suited to battle, yet they attracted recruits and, above all, served an important tactical purpose: on fields covered by the thick smoke produced by firearms and cannon using black powder, colorful uniforms served not only to distinguish one friendly regiment from another but, more importantly, friend from foe. They served also to maintain high morale and to impress the opposing forces with tall helmets and otherwise ornate headdress. In this regard armies were clothed attractively if often impractically, sacrificing comfort and function for sheer decoration. This was most apparent among senior officers who, other than the British, frequently wore uniforms of exceptional decoration, complete with silver or gold lace and plumed hats. This naturally made them easy targets for marksmen and many a general was unsaddled while leading his troops in full finery.

On campaign a soldier's uniform's natural wear and the shortage of replacement materials inevitably altered his appearance. Few troops on campaign resembled those on the parade ground back home. Indeed, in battle, the distinctions in uniform sometimes became confused by the common practice of wearing cloth or oilskin covers over helmets which, together with greatcoats and other items of campaign dress, rendered them difficult to identify at a distance. Most infantry wore their hair in a powdered pigtail, known as a 'queue', whose original purpose was to prevent long hair from impeding a man's vision. This was usually greased with candle wax, tightly twisted and tied with leather. The men were generally clean-shaven, though officers often sported moustaches. The state of hygiene was poor and lice abounded.

The infantryman, whatever his nationality, carried a considerable burden on campaign, generally consisting of a goat or calfskin leather knapsack, a leather cartridge-box, a bayonet or short saber, a canteen,

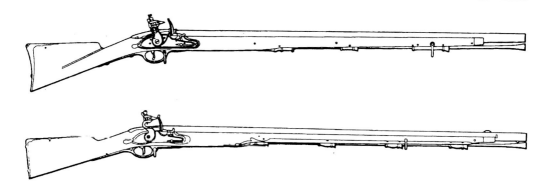

British 'Brown Bess' musket (top) and French Charleville musket (bottom). Muskets fired a simple lead ball weighing approximately an ounce which had to be rammed down the barrel after its charge in an elaborate procedure which required extensive drill to perform efficiently. To compensate for the weapon's poor accuracy, infantry were deployed shoulder to shoulder in order to concentrate their fire at opponents whose faces could often be clearly seen.

rolled greatcoat or blanket, and often a mess-tin and haversack. All this had to be firmly held in place by cross-belts and straps, balanced so as to allow the soldier to carry his 60-odd pounds – including his musket, ammunition, and rations – over great distances on the march. The infantryman's blanket or greatcoat was often rolled and worn diagonally across his body to protect against the slash of a cavalry saber or the thrust of a bayonet. If he had a particular trade, such as a cobbler or smith, he might also carry the tools of that trade. Europeans of the time were, of course, somewhat smaller than they are today, and even when one considers that the Russians were known for their large stature, the weight carried by soldiers of this period was considerable.

Boots were a fundamentally important part of a soldier's kit. The cliché that armies march on their stomachs should not allow us to forget that, whatever the importance of provisions, without proper footwear the soldier endured great hardship. Indeed, he often carried a spare pair of shoes or boots in his knapsack. There were, nevertheless, frequent cases in the early years of French infantry marching barefooted, which slowed the rate of march and caused not a little

discomfort to the wretched soldier. Needless to say a man soon learned what personal effects he could do without. Officers were not expected to carry such impedimenta: their equipment, apart from arms, was usually conveyed by wagon. The rate at which equipment was replaced naturally varied with each army and its location, but soldiers proved resourceful and could make up for some of their deficiencies by robbing the dead after a battle and by purchasing items from camp-followers or the local populace.

All nations organized their cavalry according to its specific function. Heavy cavalry required large, powerful horses for the important task of the mounted charge. The light cavalry employed smaller, quicker mounts for scouting, reconnaissance, and other duties, in addition to combat. Losses on campaign could be replaced by locally acquired remounts either purchased, requisitioned, or captured. The cavalry trooper carried his own equipment and that for the care of his horse, such as grooming brushes and nose-bags, packed in a valise behind the saddle. In addition to his saber, which hung at his side in a scabbard, the cavalryman usually carried a pistol or carbine.

Units of heavy cavalry in several armies wore a cuirass, a metal plate that protected the breast and sometimes the back as well. Body armor could not stop a musket ball, except at extreme range, but it could offer protection against saber cuts and thrusts and added an element of romantic appeal with its associations with the bygone days of chivalry. Helmets were usually made of leather, but even metal headgear seldom offered protection against the determined stroke of the saber. Horses, of course, required fodder, a fact that posed difficulties for the commissariat departments of every army. Daily consumption amounted to at least 10 pounds of hay, oats, barley, or other grain, but on campaign horses were often obliged to forage on whatever was available in the fields and forests.

As previously mentioned, the smoothbore musket served as the infantryman's basic weapon, together with a socket bayonet, while the cavalry relied chiefly on the saber. The injuries these caused were often horrific and if the victim did not succumb to a gunshot or sword wound, he was very likely to die from infection. Medical knowledge was rudimentary at best, there was little concept of hygiene, and there were no anesthetics beyond alcohol. Bullets were either extracted with instruments or the surgeon's fingers; if there was damage to a limb, amputation was inevitable. The account of a British soldier of the Napoleonic Wars only a few years later provides a glimpse of this dreadful, though sometimes indispensable, procedure:

They [the surgeons] were stripped to their shirts and bloody. Curiosity led me forward; a number of doors, placed on barrels, served as temporary tables, and on these lay the different subjects upon whom the surgeons were operating; to the right and left were arms and legs, flung here and there, without distinction, and the ground was dyed with blood ... Dr. Bell was going to take off the thigh of a soldier of the 50th, and he requested I would hold down the man for him ... The operation ... was the most shocking sight I ever witnessed; it lasted nearly half an hour, but his life was saved ... Outside of this place was an immense pit to receive the dead from the general hospital, which was close by. Twelve or fifteen bodies were flung in at a time, and covered with a layer of earth, and so on, in succession, until the pit was filled. Flocks of vultures already began to hover over this spot.

The weapons, equipment and personal effects of the dead sometimes fell to the civilian looters who often scoured the field after the action, or into the hands of comrades or enemy soldiers, depending on who held possession of the field.

A midshipman in the Royal Navy: William Henry Dillon

William Henry Dillon was born in August 1780, the illegitimate son of a middle-class family of Irish descent. His mother died in his infancy and his father, not wishing William to join a profession, sent him into the navy in 1790 at the age of 10. When Britain entered the French Revolutionary Wars in 1793 he already had three years' experience at sea, having served aboard HMS *Saturn*, a 74-gun ship-of-the-line. He was still only 13, but a midshipman nonetheless, now aboard the frigate *Thetis*.

Dillon's wartime experiences were exceptionally wide. He served on convoy and blockade duty; he was involved in the search of neutral vessels for war contraband; he visited practically every West Indian island under British, and many others under enemy, control. He witnessed mutinous behavior, punishments aboard ship, and men growing sick from tropical disease. He fought in two major and many minor naval engagements, was wounded in battle, was injured several times in the ordinary course of duty, and fell ill from fatigue and disease. He had first-hand experience of capturing enemy ships and, like all his contemporaries, eagerly sought the prize-money that these represented.

Dillon's memories of his campaigns may have gained a little luster with the benefit of hindsight, but in general they provide a fascinating insight into life at sea during the French Revolutionary Wars. Among the countless anecdotes that fill his memoirs Dillon vividly recalls the rite of passage through which all seaman crossing the 'Equinoctial line', or Equator, underwent. There was the obligatory appearance of Neptune and his 'myrmidons', who put the uninitiated through a series of unpleasant dunkings, the whole episode enlivened with music and drink. The account Dillon gives of a seaman's life aboard ship is of a hard, often monotonous existence and, apart

Sir William Henry Dillon (1780–1857) at the age of 72, one year before he reached the rank of Vice-Admiral of the Red. He spent six decades on active service in the Royal Navy, in the course of which time he produced a wealth of letters which eventually became the basis for his memoirs. (Lithograph by Bauginet, National Maritime Museum)

from the strenuous task of working the rigging and navigation, men passed countless hours with nothing to see on the horizon and the prospect of weeks at sea with only such entertainment as they could devise for themselves: cards, singing, dancing, carving, drinking.

The rigors of long years at sea often took their toll on a man's health. In the first year of the war Dillon lived for several months on salt meat without so much as a piece of fruit. 'I was obliged to be very careful in my diet, as symptoms of the scurvy had begun to show itself in my legs,' he recalled many years later. Living conditions on board were at best basic and sometimes barely tolerable. For some months black ants infested his ship, attacking anything edible before they finally sprouted wings and disappeared without a trace. The cockroaches, lice, rats, and other vermin remained on board.

Some months later Dillon was transferred to the *Defence*, a 74-gun ship-of-the-line, under Captain Gambier, who received Dillon well and promised him that 'if you attend to your duty, you will find a friend in me.' Patronage was all-important in the navy, and throughout his career Dillon always kept this in mind. In September 1793, the *Defence* joined the Channel Fleet under Lord Howe, the navy's most distinguished admiral, who had made his reputation in the War of American Independence. Discipline, hard work, attention to duty, and a strict code of morality were the order of the day aboard the *Defence*, whose seamen privately referred to their captain as 'Preaching Jemmy'. Dillon recalled how Gambier

evinced a determination to enforce his religious principles on board the ship under his command. He had prayers in his cabin twice a day, morning and evening. I was obliged to attend every morning ... As I had no Bible, he obliged me to provide myself with one, and he did not fail to examine as well my book of prayers, at the same time asking many questions upon religious subjects.

Of the 25 ships-of-the-line in Howe's fleet in the spring of 1794, the *Defence* was the first vessel involved in the first major naval engagement of the wars known as the Battle of the Glorious First of June. Dillon, still only 14 at the time, commanded three of the lower deck guns. Initial contact with the French was made on 29 May and on receiving the signal to chase the crew grew eager for the opportunity to come to grips with the enemy: 'No one thought of anything else than to exert himself to his utmost ability in overcoming the enemy,' Dillon recalled. 'Death or Victory was evidently the prevailing feeling.' Shots soon came flying over the quarter deck, killing one man and wounding nine. The captain was nearly hit, but after recovering his

Naval punishment. Captains in the Royal Navy frequently made use of flogging in answer to drunkenness, insubordination, or laziness. The offender was secured by his wrists and thighs to a grating and given a specified number of lashes ranging from a dozen to several hundred. The cat-o'-nine-tails, wielded by a boatswain's mate, quickly reduced a seaman's bare back to a bloody pulp. (Print by George Cruikshank, Ann Ronan Picture Library)

composure after a shot whistled past him he calmly removed a piece of biscuit from his pocket and began to eat it. 'He had evidently been shook by the wind of the shot. He had on a cocked hat, and kept walking the deck, cheering up the seamen with the greatest coolness.' But as casualties mounted, so too did damage to the ship, and just as the wounded were being taken below and the first fatalities thrown overboard, 'a volley of shot assailed the Poop, cut away the main brace, and made sad havoc there.'

Dillon witnessed with shock the death of a seaman in action. 'It was a most trying scene. A splinter struck him in the crown of the head, and when he fell the blood and brains came out, flowing over the deck.' But this was just the beginning; two days later the main action took place. At dawn the rival fleets were shrouded in heavy mist, but as the sun gradually broke through, visibility was restored and the great, floating engines of war, their canvas sails billowing in the wind, offered an impressive spectacle to the opposing crews. 'The weather became fine, and we enjoyed

The lower deck relaxing in harbor. As men were liable to desert if given shore leave, some captains turned a blind eye to Admiralty regulations and allowed women to come aboard. Dillon's captain took a stricter view: 'The first act was to ascertain whether all women on board were married. All their certificates were demanded … those that had not contrived to manufacture a few. This measure created a very unpleasant feeling amongst the tars.' (National Maritime Museum)

one of the most splendid sights ever witnessed – the two Fleets close to each other in line of battle, only waiting for the signal to commence the work of destruction …'

Howe's ships slowly closed on the French, and when the enemy was 10 miles off to leeward Dillon was roused from a brief slumber and summoned to his station on the lower deck. Up went the colors and the gun ports; his crews rammed home powder and shot, ran out the guns and impatiently awaited the signal to issue the first broadside. 'We retained our fire till in the act of passing under the Frenchman's stern, then, throwing all our topsails aback, luffed up [put the bow to windward] and poured in a most destructive broadside. We heard most distinctly our shot striking the hull of the enemy. The carved work over his stern was shattered to pieces.'

As the battle raged with increasing ferocity the toll began to mount. Dillon witnessed one of the crew killed by a shot that cut his head in two. At 10.30 the mizzen mast came down and the *Defence* began to drift to leeward. An hour later the main mast collapsed across the starboard side of the poop deck with a tremendous crash, and all the while, on the lower deck, where Dillon continued to shout commands above the din of roaring cannon, smoke billowed everywhere from the fire of the guns, making it almost impossible to see. The crews kept up the pace of fire so rapidly that the guns began to overheat and on recoiling they nearly struck the upper deck beams. The risk of the guns bursting became so great that Dillon ordered the crews to use less powder and lengthen the intervals between discharges.

Naval ordnance. In addition to the standard projectile – round shot – guns fired several versions of chain shot, which when leaving the barrel expanded in order to shred sails and cut and tangle rigging. Heated shot were used to set ships on fire, while grapeshot proved ideal for anti-personnel purposes, especially repelling boarders or sweeping the enemy's decks. Except at very close range only round shot possessed the power to penetrate the thick planking of a ship's hull. (Angus Konstam)

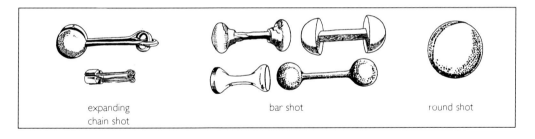

expanding   bar shot   round shot
chain shot

Battle of the Glorious First of June, 1794. While Dillon
was involved in his own drama aboard the *Defence*, at the
same time an event of an altogether different nature was
taking place aboard the *Tremendous*, another 74, where a
Mrs. McKenzie was giving birth in the midst of the
fighting. Fifty-four years later Daniel Tremendous McKenzie
was awarded the Naval General Service Medal, with a
clasp inscribed '1st June 1794'. He is almost certainly the
only man ever to have received a decoration for services
rendered as a new-born. (Roger-Viollet)

After over an hour and a half of furious
activity the men were growing weary. Often
stripped to the waist, wide-eyed with
excitement or terror, barefoot and covered in
black powder, blood, and sweat, gun crews
must have looked dreadful. Keeping these poor
wretches at the guns and working them to
maximum efficiency was the responsibility of
the officers, one of whom, on sensing signs of
fatigue, drew his sword and, brandishing it in
the air, threatened to 'cut the first man down
that did not do his duty.' On being satisfied
with their replies he returned his weapon to its
scabbard and the men resumed their fire.

Immediately afterward Dillon and two
other men were blown down from the wind
of a shot. 'I thought myself killed, as I
became senseless, being jammed between
these men.' Dillon was lucky to survive, but
the others were dead; no sooner was he back
on his feet with the help of his men than
there came a call to repel boarders. Yet battle
is a constantly fluid experience, an ever-
changing drama full of the unexpected, and
in the end the enemy vessel passed the

Defence, the immediate threat subsided, and
the order was cancelled. The French, at last,
had been beaten and were making off. At a
cost of 1,100 men Howe had captured six
enemy vessels and inflicted 3,500 casualties.

When the fighting had ended Dillon must
have been a pitiful sight. His clothes were
soaked through from water that had burst
through a port during the action, his shoes
were covered in blood, and his face and hands
smeared with burnt powder. Fourteen of the
men under his command had been either
killed or wounded and one gun had been
disabled. After shaking hands with the men to
congratulate them on their survival, he went
to the quarter deck, which he found covered
in musket shot from enemy marksmen. Below
deck, the surgeon reported the ship's losses:
91 killed and wounded, a heavy toll. Dillon
concluded, mournfully: 'The number of men
thrown overboard that were killed, without
ceremony, and the sad wrecks around us
taught those who, like myself, had not before
witnessed similar scenes that War was the
greatest scourge of mankind.'

Later in the year, aboard the *Prince George*,
Dillon went to the West Indies. This was not
a popular destination. The other
midshipmen 'were talking of nothing else
but the yellow fever. Indeed, death stared
them in the face.' But Dillon stayed on,
anxious to 'see the world', gain experience,
and, above all, to achieve promotion
through active service. He sensibly prepared
his will, well aware that the West Indian
climate and insect-borne diseases accounted
for thousands of lives every year.

Dillon went on to take part in numerous
landing operations, as well as in the siege
and capture of St Lucia in 1796, after which
he was promoted to acting lieutenant. At
Antigua he watched as sickness spread
among the ships' crews. 'Violent vomiting
attacked our seamen, the witnessing of
which was truly distressing, as they brought
up large worms.' He himself fell ill, probably
with sunstroke, which left him 'in a state of
stupefaction' for four days. He was fortunate
to recover, for various diseases, especially
yellow fever, ravaged British ships in climates

too harsh for the delicate dispositions of Europeans. There were compensations, however, and in the course of his years in the West Indies Dillon assisted in the capture of numerous prizes – mostly merchantmen and privateers – which over the years earned for him a respectable share of prize money. On one occasion he won about £20, while on another – with the capture of a valuable merchant vessel – he earned several hundred pounds. Considering his pay was only about £2 a month, this was equal to many years' ordinary income, and some fortunate men – particularly the captain and other officers, who received a disproportionately high share – could retire on such proceeds.

In 1798, while stationed in Irish waters aboard an armed cutter, he was able to take a small part against the rebellion there, storming a rebel fort with cutlass in hand and later apprehending one of the principal rebel leaders. He returned to the Jamaica Station in April 1799 and served again throughout the West Indies for the remainder of the war, taking more prizes, including a 12-gun brig whose French crew had mutinied and taken their captain prisoner. When the captain attempted to blow up the ship by taking a candle to the magazine Dillon claims to have seized him and saved the ship – and himself.

Shortly after the end of the war he went to London to see his father, who had scarcely seen his son in 12 years. Now 22, deeply tanned, and wearing plain clothes, Dillon was at first unrecognizable. His homecoming was a joyous one. 'The war was over,' he wrote in his memoirs. 'I had had twelve years of toil and anxiety.' But he could not know that the peace was to be very brief and the country would soon need him back at sea. He spent the remainder of his career on active service, including several years as a prisoner of the French and, after the Napoleonic Wars, commanding ships in several South American navies. He was knighted and retired a vice-admiral. While Dillon's experiences cannot be said to typify those of an ordinary sailor aboard ship – as such men were almost always illiterate and first-hand accounts are rare – Dillon's junior rank nevertheless placed him in close contact with ordinary ratings and his memoirs certainly give us a fascinating insight into what life must have been like.

Naval close combat. Ships locked together by tangled rigging or by deliberate grappling usually led to desperate hand-to-hand encounters between their crews. Boarding parties and defenders could choose from a wide variety of edged weapons including pikes, cutlasses, swords, dirks, and axes. Firearms, such as pistols, blunderbusses, and muskets were of more limited use, there being no time to reload them in the heat of a melee. Nevertheless, even after discharge they could still be wielded as clubs. (Roger-Viollet)

The impact of conflict

War had an immediate and direct impact on French civilians and on the populations occupied by the armies of republican France. At home, the *levée en masse* called on all citizens – men, women, and children – to contribute to the war effort. Their labor, skills, and resources – money, homes, animals, and so on – were to be requisitioned by local and national authorities as required. Thus, the decree declared:

The public buildings shall be turned into barracks, the public squares into munitions factories, the earthen floors shall be treated with lye to extract saltpetre [essential to the production of gunpowder]. All firearms of suitable calibre shall be turned over to the troops ... All saddle horses shall be seized for the cavalry; all draft horses not employed in cultivation will draw the artillery and supply wagons.

Yet if French cities and farms suffered from the loss of large numbers of their men to the army, the implications for those living in towns and villages over the border were perhaps even more painful. The fact that French armies were no longer fettered by a dependence on great supply trains and depots like their pedestrian adversaries meant that they were required to forage on occupied land. Government officials in Paris had, moreover, every reason to keep the armies of the Republic off French soil and at a safe distance from political intrigue in Paris.

The French conveniently came to justify occupation as 'liberation', a term which quickly lost its appeal to the poor inhabitants who grimly suffered the consequences. Cambon, the French Minister of Finance, said of Holland in February 1793: 'War causes misfortunes to the nations for the moment, but they are well recompensed by the establishment of liberty and equality ...

You will give to the Batavians of the poorest class the means of dancing round the tree of liberty.' Fine words, but in reality it could mean anything between heavy taxation, requisitioning, and outright pillaging.

Indeed, however enlightened the revolutionary ideas instilled in the minds of the typical republican soldier may have been, he was by no means always well disposed to the civilians into whose midst he was sent. When senior officers demanded requisitions from the local populace it naturally fell to the ordinary soldiers to perform the distasteful task of actually collecting crops, livestock, food, or whatever else the army required. This, needless to say, hardly endeared the soldiers to the local population. Words such as 'liberation' and 'liberty' rang rather hollow in the ears of the German, Belgian, and Italian peasants who saw their crops and livestock carried off with little or no compensation, their homes sometimes looted, and their pockets taxed to increase the power of the occupier. If the wars earlier in the century had not been entirely 'limited' by the stricter standards of conduct they had imposed on European armies, at least they had inflicted far less suffering on civilians than would those of the Revolutionary Wars.

Bonaparte was rather better than most revolutionary generals at compensating farmers for their crops and keeping his men under restraint, but in the end the army had to be fed; his grandiose proclamations to the peoples whose lands he was soon to despoil probably soothed few who paid any notice. 'Peoples of Italy!' he declared in April 1796, 'The French army is coming to break your chains; the French people are the friend of all peoples. So, come to receive it! Believe us, we have no grudge except against the tyrants who oppress you.'

Invading armies, whether they remained on foreign soil for long or not, sometimes posed even greater threats to the inhabitants, including rape, atrocities, and retribution meted out against civilians who violated the laws of war by offering armed resistance. On reaching the shores of Egypt in 1798 Bonaparte warned his troops against depredation:

The people of the countries where we are going treat their women differently … but in all countries, the man who rapes a woman is a monster. Looting enriches but a few. It dishonours us, it destroys our resources and it turns the people we want to befriend into our enemies.

Yet even when troops conducted themselves with a degree of self-restraint, the nastiest aspects of war occasionally arose. For those campaigning in Egypt – far from home and against an enemy of whose culture the common soldier had little understanding – atrocity and counter-atrocity were probably inevitable. No more horrendous example of this can be found than the fall of Jaffa in March 1799, when a dreadful retribution awaited its inhabitants – soldiers and civilians alike. 'The soldiers' fury was at its height,' Bonaparte reported. 'Everybody was put to the sword. Being sacked, the town experienced all the horrors of a city taken by storm.'

The French were not alone in bringing war to civilians. In the summer of 1794 Austrian troops issued an ominous warning to the residents of a village on the Luxembourg border, declaring that they would no longer ignore the wanton destruction caused by their enemies. 'Remember,' they said, 'that so far we, though victorious, have always spared the peaceful dwellings of the inhabitants of a country we are trying to liberate from the hateful slavery into which it was thrown by the regicidal Convention.' But hereafter, they continued, the French would pay for the damage done by their troops:

We swear that we, tired of the atrocities your soldiers commit every day, will no longer restrain

ourselves; every time and as many times as these villains burn down just one of our villages, we shall burn to the ground ten others in your country.

Inevitably the impact of war was greatest on inhabitants of those countries on whose land the battles were actually fought. In countries such as Britain, apart from those families who gave up a son or husband for foreign service, life carried on largely as before in a nation mercifully protected by geography and generously provided for by a thriving economy.

The economic impact of the Revolutionary Wars was felt in a number of ways in Britain. Some events were merely coincidental. Just as several military developments coincided with the conflict, so too did economic developments such as the mechanization of cotton spinning, the early development of the factory system, and the rapid expansion of canal-building. The wars also coincided with a period of considerable acceleration in population growth. While the wars might reasonably have led to a severe interruption of British trade, in fact the Royal Navy's supremacy on the seas ensured that, though trade with the Continent was disrupted by military operations, the French never managed to sever Britain's trading links with Europe, even after the occupation of Belgium and Holland in 1795 and Spain's defection to the French in 1796. The dark days of Napoleon's continental blockade were still to come.

Although the volume of British exports dropped between 1792 and 1797, it increased substantially again from 1798 to 1802, such that the overall rate of growth in the decade of war was only one percent lower than that of the preceding decade of peace. In re-exports – that is, the re-exportation of goods produced in the colonies or in foreign countries – the rate of growth was substantial, doubling in volume what it had been during the decade of peace. The volume of imports, on the other hand, grew only marginally. The 1790s were for the most part years of prosperity for Britain's trade.

Nevertheless, the picture was not entirely rosy for ordinary people, for the war years saw

Bedlam Furnace in Shropshire. Many factors contributed to making Britain the birthplace of industrialization, including good climate, technological innovation – particularly the steam engine, with which James Watt first powered machinery in 1781 – the availability of good ports through which raw materials and manufactured goods could pass and large domestic reserves of coal and iron. By 1797, Britain was exporting her surplus of iron and was far outstripping the rest of Europe in coal production. (The Tate Britain)

a gradual rise in inflation with a particularly negative impact on agricultural prices. Prices in general, but especially for food, fluctuated markedly during the war, partly due to crop failures resulting from poor weather. In 1800, for instance, prices were 40 percent higher than those only two years before. Food riots were not infrequent in these years, yet, despite rising prices and the rapid rate of population growth, imports could almost always make good the shortage of food – not the least of many benefits derived from supremacy at sea and exclusive access to small, but nevertheless fertile, colonies.

War for the British people was certainly never the all-absorbing experience that it became for the French, and even the rising demands for men to satisfy the needs of the armed forces did not place undue strain on the economy. The increased demands for men caused no serious *general* labor shortage, though some areas suffered temporarily from the loss of farmworkers and unskilled laborers – the main source of manpower for the army

and navy. Naturally the government placed more orders for food, horses, fodder, textiles, leather, and iron – but the needs of war were strictly limited and the nation and the empire could and did supply all such commodities without hardship to ordinary people. The middle class had even less reason for complaint. In Jane Austen's large personal correspondence of the time, the war is conspicuous by its absence. Although the Royal Navy does feature in her writings, scarcely a single reference to the conflict or its impact on her family's sheltered middle-class existence is made. While she remarks on the activities of the militia and a few members of the regular forces, one would otherwise assume that Britain was at peace.

Oddly, the wars did not radically increase the pace of industrialization as might be expected. Rather, they increased the prominence of agriculture. This resulted in a rise in enclosures during the 1790s so that more arable land could come under cultivation to feed the needs not merely of a rising population but also of a growing military establishment whose enlisted men ate better than their social counterparts in civilian life. Agricultural production also increased because labor shortages stimulated improvements in farm machinery, such as the threshing machine. But the simple fact remained that, unlike the highly destructive, industrially dependent conflicts of the 20th century, war in the 1790s required considerably less in the way of manufactured goods. What Britain's relatively small army needed most was food, fodder, and horses, rather than factory-produced material. Nevertheless, iron production rose to keep pace with orders for firearms and swords, the woolen industry was stimulated by the demand for uniforms, and the leather trade expanded to meet the need for shoes, horse equipment, soldiers' packs, and the like. Yet these needs never approached those of continental powers and their vast military requirements. Britain needed ships and their fittings above all else. These commodities were labor intensive and expensive but not heavily dependent on large-scale industrial production.

A cartoon published in 1796 depicting Pitt, supported by his ministers while crushing the Opposition underfoot, demonstrating his ability and determination to carry on the war against France. His right pocket holds documents indicating the large numbers of seamen, volunteers, and regular forces at the nation's disposal, while his left pocket bulges with money. A testament to Britain's financial power was its loan of £1,620,000 to Austria in 1797. (Peter Newark's Historical Sources)

Overall, the British economy grew quickly during the 1790s, enabling Pitt to institute the first income tax in 1798. Not only could the economy sustain an increasingly heavy tax burden, it also produced enough resources to continue a high rate of industrialization even where this was not essential to the war effort. Although wages fell in real terms by anything from 4 to 15 percent from their prewar levels, the standard of living remained relatively good, in spite of a rising population and higher taxes. Greater national revenue in turn translated itself into a tangible asset for war, for it enabled the government to finance the First and Second Coalitions in the form of massive subsidies and loans. If Britain could not herself field large armies, at least she could pay for those of her allies. In addition to money, Britain was a major supplier of arms. To Portugal alone in the course of five years she sent over 30,000 muskets, 11,000 carbines, 3,000 pistols, 14,000 swords, 900,000 pounds of gunpowder, 500 tons of saltpeter, 20 cannon, and £200,000 in credit. Subsidies and loans to her allies between 1793 and 1802 amounted to a staggering £15,000,000. The man in the street might grumble at the higher duties he paid on consumer goods in order to fund the war, but by and large he was in a position to afford them.

On the whole, then, the British economy weathered the Revolutionary Wars rather well and the standard of living remained, by contemporary continental standards, high. Great improvements in agriculture kept the country fed; in spite of some temporary slumps, industrial production amply supplied military and naval needs; progress in technology was not materially hindered; banks had sufficient funds to lend to investors and the government alike; and stability in overseas trade enabled the government to levy an increasing array of consumption taxes on both domestic and imported goods without serious strain on ordinary people.

The extent to which the French Revolutionary Wars may have hindered

scientific and cultural developments in
Europe is, of course, impossible to measure,
but the records of the 1790s show no lack of
cultural or scientific activity. On the
contrary, the period was quite active in the
fields of technology, medicine, exploration,
art, literature, and music. Thomas Paine's
Rights of Man, published in 1792, stands out
among a number of important political
works produced at the time. Paine continued
with his *Age of Reason* in 1794–95, while
Mary Wollstonecraft produced an early
feminist work in her *Vindication of the Rights
of Women* (1792). Thomas Malthus published
his now famous *Essay on the Principle of
Population* in 1798, while in France, Jean
Cambacérès produced a seminal legal work,
the *Projet de Code Civil* (1796), which laid the
foundation for the Napoleonic Code
introduced in 1801.

Although most of the sweeping social and
political reforms instituted by the French
came about in the early years of the
Revolution before the war commenced,
others followed, such as important
legislation that introduced compulsory
education for children turning six. In Britain,
scholarship on a higher plane reflected the
revived interest in the classical world so
prevalent in the art, fashion, and
architecture of the 1790s. In 1793, Richard
Porson, the newly appointed Professor of
Greek at Cambridge, in conjunction with
Thomas Gaisford, brought new energy to
classical studies, reflected in the publication
of Stuart and Revett's *Antiquities of Athens* in
1794.

In the field of architecture and art,
neo-classicism was at its height, as reflected
in the building of the White House in
Washington, begun in 1792 under James
Hoban, and in London, where John Soane
started work on the Bank of England in
1795. In painting, France, Spain, and Britain
all produced famous artists. David led the
way in producing grand neo-classical scenes
and images of the Revolution, such as his
famous painting of Marat lying dead in his
bath (1793). Six years later came his *Rape of
the Sabine Women*, followed by one of his

The cotton gin. Whitney's machine ended the laborious
and expensive task of separating the seeds from raw
cotton fibre in preparation for spinning. In the time it had
previously taken a slave to remove the seeds from two
pounds of cotton, the gin could raise output to a
staggering 400 pounds. Cotton production in the
American South expanded rapidly and led to
increased numbers of spinning mills in Britain.
(Ann Ronan Picture Library)

most famous works, *Napoleon Crossing the
Alps*, finished in 1801. The many art
treasures of France – as well as those looted
from abroad – found their home in the new
Louvre, which opened in 1793, a powerful
monument to national confidence. Although
they did not find their way to the British
Museum until many years later, the Elgin
Marbles arrived in London from Athens in
1801, Lord Elgin having removed them from
the Parthenon. Goya also came to the fore,
painting the *Duchess of Alba* in 1795 and
Portrait of a Woman in 1800. In Britain,
Turner painted *Millbank, Moonlight* in 1797
and *Calais Pier* in 1801.

In literature, philosophy, and music the
Germans – including Goethe, Schiller, and
Kant – were particularly productive. In
Britain the Romantic movement was
particularly influential and its focus on the
importance and inspiration of the
countryside at a time when the country was
moving toward industrialization is
particularly interesting. Wordsworth and
Coleridge published their *Lyrical Ballads* in

1798. Coleridge finished his *Kubla Khan* in 1797 (though it was not published until 1816), and Southey finished *Thalaba the Destroyer* in 1801. A number of important cultural and scientific institutions were opened at this time, including the Ecole Polytechnique in Paris in 1795, as well as the Institut National, which facilitated the study of natural science, moral and political sciences, and the arts. In music, the 1790s were a time of great productivity for Haydn, who composed many works in rapid succession, including *The Creation* in 1798 and *The Seasons* in 1801. Beethoven wrote his *Pathétique* Sonata in C Minor in 1799, and in the following year his First Symphony in C Major and his Piano Concerto No. 3 in C. In 1801, he finished his Piano Concertos Nos. 1 and 2, as well as six string quartets. The following year he wrote his 'Moonlight' Sonata and Second Symphony.

Various forms of technology emerged in the 1790s. Semaphore, invented by Claude Chappé in 1793, had an immediate military application, allowing French troops at the front to communicate rapidly with their headquarters and the British Admiralty to order ships to sea rapidly. In the same year, Eli Whitney, an American, invented his famous cotton gin, enabling the southern states to export a rapidly increasing quantity of raw cotton. Whitney went on to produce muskets with interchangeable parts in 1800, while another American launched the first submarine – the *Nautilus* – at Rouen in the same year. Medical advances included Edward Jenner's first use of vaccination against smallpox in 1796, while in 1800, the Royal College of Surgeons opened in London. Predictably, the wars interrupted the normal course of exploration, though the British continued limited expeditions, including those conducted by Mungo Park, who explored the course of the River Niger in 1795 and published his *Travels in the Interior of Africa* four years later. In 1802, Truter and Somerville explored Bechuanaland, nearly reaching Lake Ngami, while far to the east George Bass proved that Tasmania was an island, and Flinders circumnavigated Australia and mapped the coastline. While the Revolutionary Wars can be said to have dominated the decade, this brief review should serve to illustrate that life did go on and cultural movements quite separate from the war were developing.

Robert Fulton's submarine. In late 1797, the American inventor approached the French government for funds to build a machine for destroying ships at anchor using an explosive device which could be hooked to the underside of the target. The 18-foot Nautilus, with a crew of three, was completed in 1800, but by then the conservative-minded Bonaparte had taken power and refused to sanction its use. Fulton subsequently approached the Admiralty in London, which also declined his contraption. (Ann Ronan Picture Library)

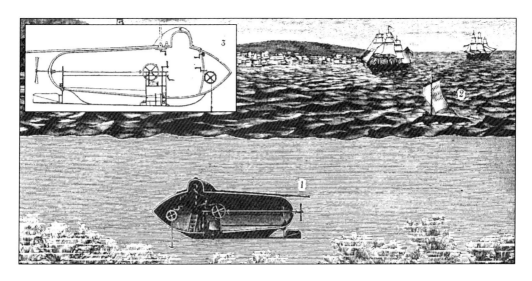

Emma Hamilton:
British Ambassadress at Naples

Emma Hamilton, who was later to become enshrined in the popular imagination through her connection with Nelson, began life in 1765 as Emily Lyon, a blacksmith's daughter from Cheshire. She first worked as a nursery-maid and on going to London in search of work became a domestic in the household of a composer. At the age of 14 she moved to a house in Arlington Street owned by a brothel-keeper known as Mrs Kelly, and appears to have become the mistress of a naval officer. It was also about this time that Emma worked in a dubious establishment where couples unable to conceive children could make use of the 'Grand celestial Bed' provided to overcome the deficiencies of infertility. At about the age of 16 she moved to the Sussex countryside and became the mistress of a gentleman of comfortable, though not extravagant, means named Charles Greville, who took her back to London and discreetly established her in Edgware Row. When Greville found for himself a rich heiress he palmed poor Emma off on his uncle, Sir William Hamilton, the Minister in Naples, and a recent widower.

Emma, together with her mother, went to Naples in 1786 and made her home at the splendid Palazzo Sessa which, being Sir William's home, doubled as the British Embassy and offered a spectacular view of the ever smoking and hissing Vesuvius. Although Emma longed to return to Greville, she soon found in Sir William a devoted admirer and a companion of undoubted social respectability. They were married while on leave in London in 1791, yet long before this Emma had become recognized in Naples for her exceptional beauty and charming manner. She soon acquired a reputation as a superb hostess and regularly dazzled a growing number of guests to Sir William's

Lady Hamilton. Emma enjoyed a charmed life at Naples, not least because of the affection she received from her husband, Sir William, to whom she was herself quite devoted. 'I am, as women generally are,' she wrote in 1794, 'ten thousand times fonder of him than I was…no quarrelling, nor crossness, nor laziness … everybody that sees us are edified by our example of conjugal and domestick felicity.' (Ann Ronan Picture Library)

parties with a singing voice which 'touched everyone's heart and whose beauty outshone that of the Venus of Medici,' as one admirer put it. She soon learned Italian, in which language she sang arias with remarkable precision and strength of feeling, to the great delight of Neapolitan high society.

Yet nothing surpassed Emma's extraordinary talent for her own form of classical drama which she styled her 'Attitudes'. On his visit to Naples Goethe described her captivating presence: With 'a beautiful face and a perfect figure,' he wrote at the time, Emma wore

a Greek costume made for her which becomes her extremely. Dressed in this, she lets down her hair and, with a few shawls, gives so much variety to her poses, gestures, expressions, etc., that the spectator can hardly believe his eyes. He sees what thousands of artists would have liked to express realized before him in movements and surprising transformations – standing, kneeling, sitting, reclining, serious, sad, playful, ecstatic, contrite, alluring, threatening, anxious, one pose follows another without a break. She knows how to arrange the folds of her veil to match each mood, and has a hundred ways of turning it into a head dress … This much is certain: as a performance it's like nothing you ever saw before in your life.

The stream of British visitors to Naples was constant, particularly in the winter. At one dinner, given to 52 guests at the Palazzo Sessa, Lady Palmerston noted that Emma's abilities more than compensated for her humble origins. She was also the particular favorite of the Neapolitan queen, Maria Carolina, the sister of the Austrian emperor. Even when Britain and Naples formed an alliance in July 1793, the outbreak of war did not stem the tide of British visitors, many of whom Emma presented at court, lodged at the Hamilton's country house at Caserta, and, of course, entertained in grand style.

The most immediate effect of the war on her life was the fact that the Anglo-Neapolitan alliance drew the Queen closer to her, and the British Ambassadress soon became a vital confidante of her 'dear dear Queen'. At the end of the year Naples' commitment to the Allies was now sought and the captain of the *Agamemnon*, Horatio Nelson, called at the Neapolitan capital on official business. Writing to his wife in admiration of the charming Ambassadress, he described her as 'a young woman of

amiable manners … who does honor to the station to which she is raised.' It was their first meeting, and they were not to meet again for another five years.

By 1795, Emma had reached a remarkable stage in life; from humble origins, no secure financial means, and no prospect of social advancement she had married an aristocrat whose profession and residence brought his talented and beautiful young wife into contact with all those on the Grand Tour of the Continent who wanted to visit a city known for high culture and an unrivaled climate. She was also the darling of the Neapolitan court.

Natural beauty and talent had served her well. Surrounded by friends and admirers, she had become the subject of numerous drawings and paintings by Romney and Gainsborough and had impressed those best placed to judge with her singing and her graceful 'Attitudes', often performed to the drama of candlelight. She had taken great pains to educate herself, as the British viceroy of Corsica noted: '… besides considerable natural understanding, she has acquired, since her marriage, some knowledge of history and of the arts, and one wonders at the application and pains she has taken to make herself what she is.' Over time, Neapolitan court politics absorbed her interest and with increasing frequency the Queen passed to Emma information useful to her husband, making her a conduit for Neapolitan documents bound for the Foreign Office in London.

The French occupation of Rome in February 1798 cast an ominous shadow over the Kingdom of Naples. Sir Horatio Nelson was to come to its aid. His star had by then risen with his exploits the previous year at the Battle of Cape St Vincent. But that was simply the start; his subsequent spectacular victory at the Nile sent Emma into paroxysms: 'How shall I begin,' ran a letter to Nelson full of overwhelming flattery, and bordering on hero-worship.

What shall I say to you? 'tis impossible I can write, for since last Monday I am delerious with joy, and assure you I have a fevour caused by agitation and pleasure. God, what a victory! Never, never has there been anything half so glorious, so compleat ... I wou'd not like to die till I see and embrace the Victor of the Nile ...

She and Sir William were rowed out to the conquering hero when he arrived at Naples in the *Vanguard*. 'Up flew her ladyship,' Nelson wrote to his wife, 'and exclaiming: "Oh God is it possible?" fell into my arms more dead than alive.'

Nelson was soon ensconced at the Hamilton's request in the upper rooms of the Palazzo Sessa and before long he was writing to his wife, describing Emma as 'one of the very best women in this world, she is an honour to her sex.' Quite when the affair between Nelson and Emma began is not known, but it may very well have begun when, soon after his arrival, a feverish Nelson collapsed from the fatigue of the preceding campaign and was nursed by Emma.

Meanwhile, the military situation grew grim. After a disastrous campaign further north, the Neapolitan army had signed an armistice with the French, who, triumphant in northern and central Italy, were now poised to occupy Naples as well. The royal family and the Hamiltons took refuge on Sicily, and it was not long before Nelson hoped to hatch a scheme to retake the mainland capital. Indeed, there were rumors that Nelson, dressed as a midshipman, and Emma, attired in masculine clothes, would walk along the marina and visit the taverns, listening to gossip and assessing the level of support for the royalist cause. Throughout the first half of 1799, Nelson continued to live with the Hamiltons, now in Palermo at the Palazzo Palagonia, an impressive building of 50 rooms. Emma, meanwhile, continued to preside over the dinners provided by the exiled British Embassy. In time Nelson's relationship with Emma began to raise eyebrows among British observers, civilian and naval alike. Lock, the Chargé d'affaires, noted with dismay 'the unbounded power her ladyship possesses over ... Lord Nelson ... The extravagant love

of the latter has made him the laughing stock of the whole fleet ...'

In mid-June 1799, Emma and Sir William left Palermo in secret for Naples, hoping to support the return of Bourbon rule. The French army had departed, having installed an unpopular republican government that was now succumbing to forces loyal to King Ferdinand. When the Hamiltons entered the Bay of Naples on 24 June the city had fallen to the fury of a royalist counter-revolution but was in such chaos that landing was considered unsafe. For six weeks they remained aboard HMS *Foudroyant*, while on shore a bitter retribution was under way for those suspected of republican sympathies or complicity with the former government. The wave of arrests in turn produced a flood of petitions, pleading protection, for Emma's consideration, for many of the accused were her friends. The whole episode was distressing, for the Hamiltons stood to lose countless friends whom Nelson had derisively called, rightly or wrongly, 'rebels, Jacobins and fools.' Some were reprieved, but most met a cruel and ignominious end when the King and Queen returned in August.

By the autumn of 1799, Emma and Nelson's infatuation for one another was plain for all to see and Lady Elgin, for one, found Emma's attachment to Nelson downright indecent, adding:

I must acknowledge she is pleasant, makes up amazingly ... She looked very handsome at dinner, quite in an undress; my Father would say, 'There is a fine Woman for you, good flesh and blood." She is indeed a Whapper! and I think her manner very vulgar. It is really humiliating to see Lord Nelson, he seems quite dying and yet as if he had no other thought than her.

Sir William, meanwhile, nearly 70 and in failing health, had received permission from the Foreign Office to retire, and in April 1800, he, Emma, and Nelson left together for the journey home. By this time Emma's infidelity was an open secret, but Sir William did not appear to disapprove; indeed, he and Nelson remained close friends throughout. They

One of the many 'Attitudes' performed by Emma. Heavy with classical allusions, such poses appealed to those of the cultured classes who steeped themselves in the study of ancient literature, sculpture, architecture, and philosophy. In Emma's day, Greek and Roman archaeological finds were of particular interest to scholars like her husband, who amassed a large collection of vases which he sent to Britain in 1798. (Roger-Viollet)

Nelson always evident. The British Ambassadress at Vienna observed that Nelson

is devoted to Emma; he thinks her quite an angel, and talks of her as such to her face and behind her back, and she leads him about like a keeper with a bear. She must sit by him at dinner to cut his meat; and he carries her pocket handkerchief.

Emma sang magnificently with Haydn before continuing on to Prague and Dresden, where still more of their hosts could see the transparent way Emma and Nelson carried on. The British minister at Dresden noted that 'it is plain that Lord Nelson thinks of nothing but Lady Hamilton, who is totally occupied by the same object ... Lady Hamilton takes possession of him, and he is a willing captive, the most submissive and devoted I have seen.' Finally, after five months, their tour of the Continent came to an end and they embarked at Hamburg at the end of October 1800.

Emma was by then seven months pregnant and her daughter, Horatia, was born the following January. By that time Nelson was back at sea, and though he left his wife in 1801 they never divorced. Sir William Hamilton died in 1803. Lady Hamilton and Nelson maintained their affair until Nelson's heroic death at Trafalgar. Devoted to the end, one of Nelson's final statements to Captain Hardy aboard the *Victory* was 'Take care of my dear Lady Hamilton.' Still legally married, and with his paternity of Horatia a close secret, Nelson could do nothing financially for Emma apart from leaving a request in his will that Parliament provide 'ample provision to maintain her rank in life.' It did not honor Nelson's wishes, for the nation was not prepared to support his mistress, however generously it would honor his wife and his memory. In time Emma squandered the money left to her by Sir William, went into serious debt, and took refuge from her creditors in France, where she died in poverty in 1814. Horatia married an English curate in 1822 and died in 1881.

cruised to Syracuse and Malta, in the course of which journey Emma conceived a child by Nelson. They eventually landed at Leghorn, on the Italian coast, and proceeded by land, narrowly escaping capture by the French near Ancona before continuing by ship to Trieste.

On entering Austrian territory they were entertained by aristocrats and rich merchants, all by virtue of Nelson's presence. Cheered and applauded wherever they went, especially in Vienna, where they stayed for six weeks, the Hamiltons and Nelson attended a constant stream of operas, concerts, dinners, and receptions, with Emma's affection for

Hohenlinden and Copenhagen

Although the Battle of Marengo was a magnificent military achievement and a victory that would forever be close to Bonaparte's heart, it did not quite toll the death knell of the Second Coalition. After Marengo, Austrian and French negotiators had opened talks for peace, but when these failed and the truce ended on 13 November, hostilities resumed on the Rhine front. There, the new, inexperienced Austrian Commander-in-Chief, Archduke John, led a respectable force of 120,000 men, but morale was low and the French could oppose them with Moreau's 180,000 troops, based around Munich. Poor weather and administrative

The Battle of Copenhagen, 2 April 1801. Formed in line ahead, Nelson's fleet (center) engages Danish vessels, floating batteries and land defenses. Three hours into the action he sent an ultimatum ashore which led to a ceasefire: 'If the firing is continued on the part of Denmark, Lord Nelson will be obliged to set on fire all the floating batteries he has taken without having the power of saving the brave Danes who have defended them.' (Painting by Nicholas Pocock, National Maritime Museum)

problems meant that John only began his advance at the River Inn on November 29, and while he managed to begin a wide flanking movement around his opponent's northern flank, Moreau was in turn threatening John's left, in the direction of Vienna. This obliged the Austrians to proceed east against Munich, thus threatening Moreau's base while simultaneously protecting Vienna. As a result of these maneuvers the two armies met about 20 miles east of the Bavarian capital, in the depths of the Hohenlinden Forest, where the last great land battle of the Revolutionary Wars now took place.

On 2 December the Austrians probed but failed to penetrate the defenses Moreau had established on both sides of the main road that led into the city. On the following day, however, John attacked in considerable force, exerting great pressure on Ney in the center, while on the French right, General Richepanse took matters into his own hands and assailed the Austrian left wing, driving it

Jean Victor Moreau. One of the foremost French generals of the Revolutionary Wars, Moreau held senior posts on the Rhine in 1795–96 where his exceptional abilities brought him into public prominence. As Commander-in-Chief in Italy in 1799 he was defeated at Cassano before being transferred back to the Rhine front, where he achieved victory at Höchstädt a few days after Marengo. His triumph at Hohenlinden six months later knocked Austria out of the war. (Roger-Viollet)

back across rough terrain and inflicting serious losses in the process. With his assault on the French center a failure and his left in disarray, John was obliged to fall back in the direction of Vienna, and what might have been an orderly retreat soon disintegrated into a rout. The battle and subsequent withdrawal cost him 18,000 men, and though he tried to halt the French pursuit at Salzburg he was unable to stop Moreau's victorious forces, about 7,000 of whom had fallen in the fighting. While Moreau's staff urged him to follow up his success and advance on the Austrian capital itself, he himself knew the game was up. 'Without any doubt, it would be a fine thing to enter Vienna,' he said in reply to their entreaties. 'But it is a much finer thing to dictate peace.'

The Austrians, meanwhile, reviewed their situation with dismay. The Emperor Francis re-appointed Archduke Charles as Commander-in-Chief on 17 December, but even that great general could not work miracles. The army, disorganized and in desperate need of fresh troops, simply could not face another battle. Worse still, not only was Moreau poised for a drive on Vienna, but Macdonald had advanced through Switzerland and was already in the Tyrol, while Brune was moving north from Italy. Threatened from three sides and with no way of opposing this determined offensive, the Emperor authorized Charles to negotiate an armistice, which the two sides duly concluded at Steyr on Christmas Day.

The continental war was over and with it, by definition, went the Second Coalition. When the Austrian Foreign Minister, Baron Thugut, prepared instructions for the imperial envoy who was to conclude a separate peace with France, he painfully summed up the total defeat of his country:

I have written with trembling hands the unfortunate instructions that I have the honour of submitting … and which I regard as the epitaph of the Monarchy and of the glory of Austria; but His Majesty has ordered it absolutely, and one cannot contest his right to dispose of the heritage of his ancestors as he sees fit!

But if France had now cowed all *continental* resistance, Britain continued her naval war and in the spring of 1801, prepared to take on the fleets of Denmark, Sweden, and Russia – the powers forming the League of Armed Neutrality. When the Danes refused to comply with British demands, Nelson, on 2 April, attacked the anchorage at Copenhagen – 20 ships-of-the-line, supported by floating batteries and harbor forts. The fighting was exceptionally severe and when Parker wrongly concluded that Nelson faced imminent defeat he issued the signal to disengage. Nelson, being Nelson, ignored it. 'Now, damn me if I do,' he declared when asked if he saw the order, maintaining aloft his own signal for *close action*. He paced the deck greatly annoyed, shifting the stump of his right arm. Turning to the captain of his flagship, Nelson made that declaration now famous to posterity – 'You know, Foley, I have only one eye – I have a right to be blind sometimes' – and then placing a telescope up to his blind eye he announced dismissively, 'I really do not see the signal.' As Nelson declined to repeat Parker's signal the savage exchange of broadsides continued unabated.

As round shot whistled through the air, Captain Edward Riou, commanding the 38-gun frigate *Amazon*, sat perched on a gun carriage, encouraging his men. Then a raking shot fired from one of the Danish forts wounded him in the head with a splinter and killed his clerk beside him. Another shot struck a party of Marines, upon which Riou cried out, 'Come then, my boys, let us die all together!' Almost immediately another shot cut him in two. Riou, along with about 1,000 of his compatriots, were killed – together with about an equal number of Danes – but by the end of the day Nelson had nearly destroyed the entire Danish fleet and the remnant was given up after negotiations.

With the destruction of the Danish fleet, the death of Tsar Paul, and the collapse of the League of Armed Neutrality, the Anglo-French conflict could only end, by default, as a draw. At sea Britain had established undisputed command of the waves and conquered virtually the entire French colonial empire, yet was powerless to compensate for the continental advantages reaped by the revolutionary armies in the Low Countries, Germany, Switzerland, and Italy.

France was wearied by the wars spawned by revolution and fueled by her own success, and now desired peace. She labored under a number of disadvantages of her own. So long as Britain remained supreme at sea, Bonaparte was unable to re-establish a New World empire. By virtue of distance, the recent accession of the vast Louisiana territory from Spain could not be exploited, nor could France hope to recover Haiti from the native rebels who had liberated it, with British assistance, in 1801. With her overseas trade severely curtailed by British blockade and fleet

action, France found she could no longer reap the benefits which war on the Continent had provided since 1792. Finally, the death of Tsar Paul, Francophile though neutral, as well as British successes in Egypt in 1801, signaled the end of any prospect of Franco-Russian cooperation against Turkey or Britain.

In Britain calls for peace were even more pressing. By 1801, she found herself shorn of continental allies as a result of Austria's separate peace and Russia's earlier defection from the Second Coalition. The European states had, in fact, begun to turn against Britain's maritime policies of blockade and the search and seizure of neutral vessels. They would no longer tolerate her practice of exhorting the Continent to arms, accruing to herself the advantages of colonial acquisitions and overseas markets without the losses attendant upon direct operations against France. In short, while the continental powers stood to lose vast stretches of territory to France, Britain remained relatively secure from attack. Only a few enemy colonies still resisted capture, while many of the most important ports of the Continent remained closed to British trade in any event and others, still open, such as those of Portugal, were on the verge of seizure by hostile Spain. Finally, the demands of merchants from London, Lancashire, Liverpool, and elsewhere – a class of men growing in political as well as financial power – could not be ignored in Whitehall, where ministers at least privately acknowledged their desire to reopen lost trade links with France, Britain's greatest prewar market.

Thus, with Britain mistress of the seas and France supreme on land, both sides regarded further recourse to arms as futile. Protracted negotiations at Amiens ended the stalemate; a preliminary peace was signed on 1 October 1801 and, after much talk but few modifications, the final treaty was agreed on 25 March 1802, thus bringing an uneasy termination to a decade of uninterrupted war. There was general rejoicing in both countries, but that jubilation was to be short-lived, particularly in Britain.

France triumphant

At the end of hostilities, with France and Britain dominant in entirely different realms, precisely how did this historically unprecedented state of affairs translate in political terms? The political results of the French Revolutionary Wars may be traced in the two principal treaties by which that conflict came to an end.

The Treaty of Lunéville, concluded on 9 February 1801 between France and Austria, demonstrates the greatly enhanced status of France. For a start, Austria was effectively barred from most of Italy: 'The interests of Europe will not permit the Emperor to cross the Adige,' Bonaparte told the *Corps Legislatif*, adding, 'Austria ought not to expect from its defeats that which it would not have obtained by victories.' By its terms Austria confirmed her previous commitment at Campo Formio to French annexation of Belgium and her recognition of the satellite states created as a result of conquest: the Batavian (Dutch), Helvetic (Swiss), Cisalpine (northern Italian – chiefly Lombardy), and Ligurian (Genoese) Republics. Yet for his pains the Emperor Francis did not go entirely unrewarded. He kept Venice and its territories along the Adriatic and, although he had lost his traditional influence over Tuscany, his brother, Archduke Ferdinand, made small territorial gains in the form of the ecclesiastical states of Salzburg, Passau, and Berchtesgaden.

The greatest changes took place in Germany, where Austria recognized the French claim to the whole of the left bank of the Rhine, including all former Prussian territories. Furthermore, Francis agreed that secular princes who thus lost territory should be compensated with lands belonging to the ecclesiastical states. In agreeing to these terms Francis – who was, it should be remembered, not only Emperor of Austria but also the Holy Roman Emperor – was laying the basis for the final dissolution of that 1,000-year-old institution. Indeed, Lunéville set the stage for the subsequent radical re-drawing of much of western Germany in 1803, by which large numbers of small states were absorbed by larger, secular rulers, making Germany more consolidated, more Protestant, and therefore more closely connected with Prussia. This was decisive for the future of Germany as a whole, for it lent Prussia far greater prominence in German affairs than ever before, ultimately ensuring that when the cause of unification arose in the years after Waterloo it would be Prussia and not Austria who would lead the movement.

OVERLEAF
1. **Austrian Netherlands (Belgium)** Invaded, 1792; annexed, 1795; formally recognized by Austria, 1797.
2. **Holland** Invaded, 1794. Batavian Republic established, 1795.
3. **Switzerland** 'Rauracian Republic' annexed 1792; invaded, 1798; Helvetic Republic established.
4. **Nice and Savoy** Invaded 1792; annexed 1793 and 1796, respectively.
5. **Piedmont** Invaded, 1796; Piedmontese Republic established 1799.
6. **Cisalpine Republic** Established 1797 including ex-Modenese and ex-Venetian territory, plus Swiss district of Valtelline.
7. **Ligurian Republic** Established 1797 in place of Genoa, occupied since 1792.
8. **Papal States** Occupied, 1797; Roman Republic proclaimed, 1798; Papal rule restored, 1800; Concordat with France, 1801.
9. **Tuscany** Brief French occupations, 1799, 1800; transformed into Kingdom of Etruria, 1801 as Spanish possession.
10. **Venetian Republic** France divides territory between Cisalpine Republic and Austria, 1797.
11. **Kingdom of Naples** Mainland territories occupied, January 1799; Parthenopean Republic established; French withdraw, July.
12. **Parma** Occupied 1797-99.
13. **Left bank of the Rhine** Scene of fighting, 1792–97; largely under French control by 1795; annexed, 1797.
14. **Ionian Islands** Annexed from Venetian Republic, 1797.

French conquests

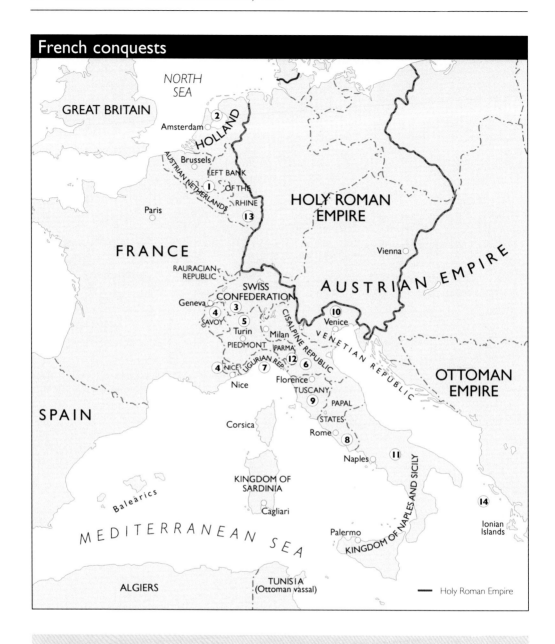

Colonial conquests restored by Britain at Amiens

Restored to Holland
Dutch Virgin Islands
St Eustatius   St Martin
St Bartholomew
Curaçao   Surinam   Demerara,
Essequibo, and Berbice
Cochin and Negapatam
Cape Colony

Restored to Spain
Minorca

Restored to France
Martinique St Lucia Tobago

Colonial conquests retained by Britain at Amiens
Ceylon (from Holland)
Trinidad (from Spain)

Europe in 1802

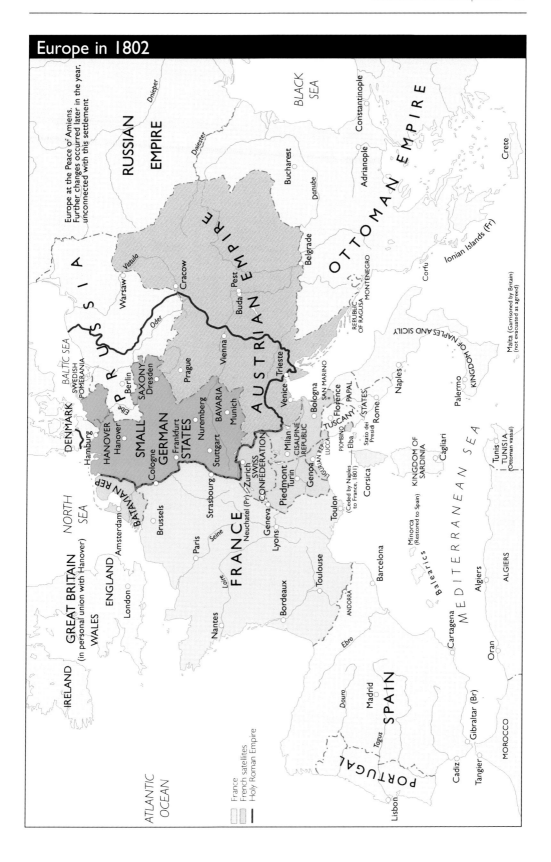

Europe at the Peace of Amiens.
Further changes occurred later in the year,
unconnected with this settlement

France
French satellites
Holy Roman Empire

PREVIOUS PAGE
Few geographical changes had occurred on the Continent in the five years since Campo Formio and neither Lunéville nor Amiens did much to change this. After her defeat of the Second Coalition France naturally retained the extraordinary gains she had made in the first half of the Revolutionary Wars, but apart from the cession of Parma by the puppet Cisalpine Republic, Lunéville was little more than a reconfirmation of Campo Formio. Amiens had even less impact on the Continent for the obvious reason that Britain was, notwithstanding Hanover, not a continental power. She formally accepted French control over Belgium, the west bank of the Rhine and northwest Italy, and in return France promised to respect the independence of Switzerland, the Papal States and Naples. Yet none of these concessions altered the map of Europe. The situation in the colonial world, however, had changed – as in Europe in favor of France and her allies.

The Treaty of Amiens, concluded between France and Britain on 25 March 1802, brought a formal end to the French Revolutionary Wars and heaped yet further advantages upon France. This agreement was nothing if not flawed, and probably numbers among the most controversial treaties ever concluded by a British government. Indeed, its weaknesses were apparent even before its signature, and together with later French provocation it laid the seeds for the renewal of war only 14 months later. 'The provisions,' wrote one British contemporary, 'were a mockery upon us, and not capable of being carried into effect. Nothing surely can be worse than loose stipulations in a treaty of peace, or such as are difficult to execute.' This expression of alarm was more than justified, for the terms were scandalously favorable to France. The key elements of the treaty stipulated that all French and Dutch overseas colonies, including the Cape of Good Hope, were to be restored by Britain. France was also to receive Elba, while Minorca and Malta were to be restored to Spain and the Knights of St John, respectively. France, for her part, agreed to evacuate the Kingdom of Naples and the Roman States, as well as Egypt (where her troops had, in any event, already been decisively defeated), which was then restored to Turkey.

Britain's extensive cessions caused alarm and despondency, particularly to Pitt, who

had only recently left office, and his supporters. With evidence seeming daily to confirm the aggressive tendencies of France, those sacrifices were being keenly felt. The surrender of strategic points around the globe prompted stinging criticism from a number of politicians. Henry Dundas, the former Secretary of State for War, wrote:

To have [retro]ceded to France, Martinique, Malta, Minorca, the Cape, the Dutch settlements both in the East and West Indies and even Cochin, and to have obtained nothing in return but the name of peace, is such an act of weakness and humiliation as nothing in my opinion can justify.

Britain was in no position to demand extensive indemnities from France, Dundas continued, 'but I hoped we would obtain security for what we got.' Amiens offered her virtually no security, only a short-lived and costly truce.

Trouble arose almost immediately, as Talleyrand, the French Foreign Minister, astutely observed: 'Hardly was the Peace of Amiens concluded, when moderation commenced to abandon Bonaparte; this peace had not yet received its complete execution before he was sowing the seeds of new wars ...' The surrender of the Cape was lamentable enough, Dundas complained, recognizing that the Cape was the key to the southern route to India, but 'we have done even worse by giving up Malta, for we have abandoned Egypt to a future danger from France and we have abandoned the proud pre-eminence we had obtained in the Mediterranean.' Malta, with its superb port of Valetta, served as the Royal Navy's vital strategic base in the central Mediterranean; its loss therefore threatened the security of the whole Mediterranean coastline.

In addition to the fatal weaknesses inherent in Amiens, the fact that Britain was not a signatory to the Treaty of Lunéville also had far-reaching consequences, most notably the great potential offered to France for territorial acquisitions on the Continent without the legal interference of Britain.

France was not required to evacuate Dutch territory or recognize the Batavian Republic's independence. Therefore the Cape of Good Hope, once again a Dutch possession, lay subject to French influence. Thus, Lunéville guaranteed independence to the French satellite states of the Helvetic, Cisalpine, and Ligurian Republics, though of course since Britain had no part in the treaty there was no sanction to prevent France from ignoring the sovereignty of these peoples. Consequently, with Austria cowed and exhausted by her defeat in numerous disastrous campaigns stretching back to 1792, the terms of Lunéville could be respected or violated at the First Consul's will without reference to Britain. It is hardly surprising, then, that contemporary British opinion regarded France as the major beneficiary of Amiens. Lord Grenville, the former Foreign Secretary, was aghast:

I consider the present treaty ... merely with reference to the question of terms, as it affects our security at home and abroad; the balance of strength, particularly of naval and colonial strength, between us and above all, the general credit and dignity of our national character. In all these points it appears to me most miserably defective; but ... it is most of all so in the last point ...

Yet the military situation seemed to ministers to leave little option but to make an accommodation with France.

Amiens soon came to be regarded as a truce rather than a conclusive pacification. George III was reported to have said of it, 'Do you know what I call the peace – an experimental peace, for it is nothing else ... It was unavoidable. I was abandoned by everybody, allies and all.' Talleyrand's assessment of the situation seems, therefore, most astute: 'It can be said without the least exaggeration that at the time of the Peace of Amiens France enjoyed abroad such power, such glory, and such influence, that the most ambitious spirit could hardly desire more for his country.' But the ambitions of the First Consul were higher than his foreign minister

or indeed anyone could have expected. France failed to follow the spirit of the Treaties of Lunéville and Amiens, continuing to look to her own territorial aggrandizement at the expense of the future peace of Europe. With hindsight it is easy to identify the shortcomings of these treaties and find in them the seeds of the Napoleonic Wars.

It is impossible to assess with any accuracy the losses sustained by each side in the wars, but battlefield losses alone accounted for many tens of thousands of French and Austrians, not to mention other nationals. We also know that, until the end of the 19th century, sickness, disease, and fatigue always accounted for several times as many deaths as losses in combat. It is known that France alone lost several hundred thousand men. British military and naval losses exceeded 100,000. Most were victims of dysentery, yellow fever, and other tropical diseases in the West Indies. There, perhaps 80,000 men died or were invalided out of the service between 1794 and 1796. Over 40 percent of the troops stationed in the Windward and Leeward Islands died of illness in 1796 alone.

Such losses might have been avoided had the Great Powers combined forces from the start and appreciated the enormous political, social, and military threat which revolutionary France posed as a catalyst for upheaval elsewhere and as a renegade power willing and, as events soon proved, able to smash the existing balance of power in Europe. In addition to the distractions caused by the two final partitions of Poland in 1793 and 1795, the Allies had squandered the opportunity of defeating revolutionary France by failing to combine their forces in one great coalition – a mistake they would continue to repeat until 1813 when, at last, all Europe opposed an enemy fatally weakened by years of campaigning, highlighted by disaster in Russia and Spain. At the beginning of the wars the forces of the various German states of the Holy Roman Empire alone, had they been put in the field, would have exceeded 600,000 men. Yet even without these, the combined might of Austria, Prussia, and Russia, operating on

Major actions at sea (1793-1801) and strength of forces 1790

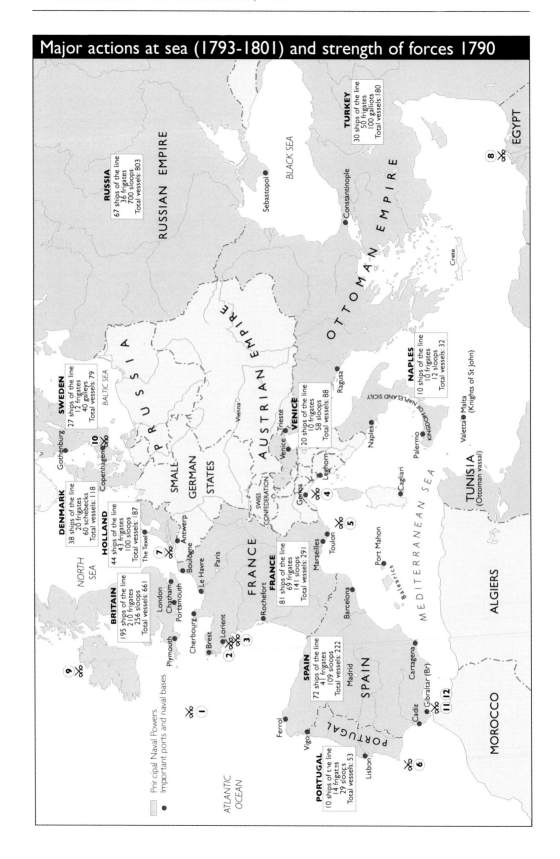

RUSSIA
67 ships of the line
36 frigates
700 sloops
Total vessels: 803

TURKEY
30 ships of the line
50 frigates
100 galliots
Total vessels: 180

SWEDEN
27 ships of the line
12 frigates
40 galleys
Total vessels: 79

DENMARK
38 ships of the line
20 frigates
60 schebecks
Total vessels: 118

HOLLAND
44 ships of the line
43 frigates
100 sloops
Total vessels: 187

BRITAIN
195 ships of the line
210 frigates
256 sloops
Total vessels: 661

FRANCE
81 ships of the line
69 frigates
141 sloops
Total vessels: 291

SPAIN
72 ships of the line
41 frigates
109 sloops
Total vessels: 222

PORTUGAL
10 ships of the line
14 frigates
29 sloops
Total vessels: 53

VENICE
20 ships of the line
10 frigates
58 sloops
Total vessels: 88

NAPLES
10 ships of the line
10 frigates
12 sloops
Total vessels: 32

Principal Naval Powers
Important ports and naval bases

OPPOSITE

1. **Glorious First of June, 1 June 1794** - The first major naval encounter proves an important morale boast for Britain, but Howe fails to stop a vital grain convoy from reaching France.

2. **Belle Ile, 17 June 1795** - Outnumbered Cornwallis skillfully escapes from a superior French force.

3. **Ile de Groîx, 23 June 1795** - Bridport defeats Villaret off Ile de Groix.

4. **The Gulf of Genoa, 13–14 March 1795**

5. **Hyéres, 13 July 1795** - Hotham fights indecisive actions off Genoa and Toulon.

6. **St Vincent, 14 February 1797** - Jervis, aided by Nelson's exceptional boldness, decisively defeats the Spanish and prevents them from combining with the French for an invasion of Britain.

7. **Camperdown, 11 October 1797** - Duncan, with 16 ships, fights a bitter contest against 15 Dutch, capturing nine of them.

8. **The Nile, 1 August 1798** - Nelson, with 14 sail, utterly defeats Brueys, leaving the French stranded in Egypt and restoring British control of the Mediterranean.

9. **Donegal, 12 October 1798** -Warren defeats a squadron carrying French troops off Ireland.

10. **Copenhagen, 2 April 1801** - Nelson, with 12 ships, destroys the Danish fleet at anchor, ending the League of Armed Neutrality.

11–12. **Algeciras I and II, 6, 12–13 July 1801** - Saumarez, initially checked, defeats a superior Franco-Spanish force.

several mutually supporting fronts, would certainly have put paid to the Revolution long before the *levée en masse* took such decisive effect and before the emergence of the man who was to shape the destiny of France – and much of the Continent as well – until 1815. Instead, the Allies fought piecemeal, dividing their armies and efforts to challenge their opponents at different points with insufficient force and predictable results.

What did the French Revolutionary Wars accomplish and what was their legacy? Far and away the most significant result was the preservation and consolidation of the Revolution itself. None of the products and achievements of this, the most important political and social movement in modern history, would have survived had France suffered early defeat. Constitutional government, a limited franchise, secularization of the state, wholesale social and judicial reforms, the elimination of aristocratic and clerical privileges, and the abolition of feudalism, all stemmed from the French Revolution. In urban areas it granted new political power to the middle class, while in the countryside it transferred vast tracts of church, crown and aristocratic land to the peasantry. All of these changes owed their existence to the Republic's success in the field.

Yet the impact of the Revolution was hardly limited to France; indeed, it fundamentally changed Europe. In spite of Jacobin radicalism, many Europeans plainly recognized that the Revolution symbolized popular sovereignty and equality before the law. It was the first time, moreover, that an entire people became identified with the Nation. Above all, the success of the armies of the Revolution meant that liberalism and nationalism – the two central features of the 19th century – would not only survive, but flourish.

When we assess the French Revolutionary Wars we must try to avoid swallowing whole all the stereotypes and mythologies associated with it. Strictly speaking, the French Revolution was not the birthplace of nationalism. Even in the absolute monarchy of Frederick the Great, Prussians were beginning to fight not merely on behalf of their king, but on behalf of a nation which, while not embracing a pan-German philosophy, at the very least viewed the French as hereditary enemies. Here, through the upheaval of war, were the beginnings of national identity, a process rapidly accelerated by, but not strictly invented by, the French Revolution and the wars which sprang from it.

Nor can it be said that revolutionary warfare began with the French Revolutionary Wars – at least not in the main. It is certain that they sped the process of change already underway. Building on existing military thought, French military commanders employed revolutionary tactics against their hidebound royal counterparts with remarkable success. The origins of revolutionary warfare are, however, to be found in the innovations and reforms resulting from the experience of battle both in Europe and in North America in the decades which immediately preceded the general European war to which the French Revolution gave rise. However ably the generals of the Revolution wielded these principles, it may not be said that they *created* them. Napoleon Bonaparte proved exceptional, of course, and his strategic genius helps us divine the break between the wars of maneuver and the wars of decisive encounters.

War, as Clausewitz later wrote in *On War*, was now about destroying the enemy's armed forces through direct confrontation on the battlefield, having first placed oneself in the most advantageous position. Hereafter, war meant *seeking* direct confrontation between contending forces rather than deliberately avoiding it, thus hoping to achieve a decisive result. Combatants in the field also grew to numbers previously unheard of in European history, for the principle of the 'Nation in Arms' meant that those countries who chose to embrace this idea could hereafter wield forces of unprecedented size. The age of modern warfare had dawned.

If the French Revolutionary Wars created the greatest general, they also produced the greatest admiral. In the annals of naval warfare Nelson stands alone. To be fair, while Napoleon ranks first among great military commanders, he at least has had some illustrious company over the centuries. By the end of the French Revolutionary Wars Nelson was nearly broken in health and bore for all to see the scars of years of arduous duty at sea and the wounds of close combat. He had won two brilliant victories at the Nile and at Copenhagen, and it only remained for him to complete the trinity with his last and greatest triumph at Trafalgar in 1805 – so decisive a victory that Britannia truly *did* rule the waves for the next 100 years.

On land, as well, the French Revolutionary Wars produced battles of great significance, both politically and tactically. Valmy, being little more than an exchange of cannon fire, hardly even qualifies as a battle,

but from a political point of view it was immensely important: it saved the newly born Republic, signed the death warrant of Louis XVI and Marie Antoinette (with the great political implications this had for Anglo-French relations), enabled France to conquer Belgium and the Rhineland, and transformed what everyone imagined would be a short war into an epic worldwide struggle which lasted for over two decades. Then there was Fleurus in 1794, which effectively ensured that France would retain control of the Low Countries – which indeed it did for the next 20 years. At Castiglione in 1796, Bonaparte's tactical abilities resulted in a spectacular double envelopment, while throughout the campaigns of 1796–97 he continuously demonstrated the decisive results to be achieved by dividing his enemy's forces before defeating them in detail. Later, at Marengo in 1800, Bonaparte refused to accept initial defeat and took advantage of the Austrians' slow pursuit operations to reorganize his forces, receive reinforcements, and deliver, after concentrating his artillery fire, an effectively conceived and executed counterattack.

The French Revolutionary Wars not only produced in Napoleon Bonaparte history's greatest military commander; on the basis of his military successes and his extraordinary personal charisma, the wars also thrust him into the political limelight, enabling him to occupy the same role as his monarchical rivals – supreme leader of the army as well as of the state – even if that state was still a republic in name. Thus, paradoxically, a conflict meant to spread republicanism and liberty in fact left France under dictatorial rule born of a coup. That dictatorship, having been forged on the battlefields of Italy and Egypt, had by definition no basis in political legitimacy. Napoleon would not be satisfied until he was not just First Consul but also Emperor of France. Thus, only through further victories could a self-appointed emperor hope to sustain himself in power – and therein lay the basis for the early renewal of hostilities in a yet greater and more destructive contest of arms, the Napoleonic Wars.

Further reading

Barthorp, M., *Napoleon's Egyptian Campaigns, 1798–1801* (London, Osprey 1978).

Bertaud, J., *The Army of the French Revolution* (Princeton, Princeton University Press repr. 1988).

Blanning, T.C.W., *The Origins of the French Revolutionary Wars* (London, Longman repr. 1997).

–*The French Revolutionary Wars* (London, Arnold, 1976).

Chandler, D., *The Campaigns of Napoleon* (New York, MacMillan,1966).

Clausewitz, Carl von, *On War* (ed. and trans. M. Howard and P. Paret, Princeton, Princeton University Press, 1983).

Dillon, W.H., *Dillon's Narrative*, I (London, Navy Records Society, 1953).

Duffy, C., *Eagles across the Alps* (Chicago, The Emperor's Press, 1998).

Elting, J.R., *Swords around a Throne* (London, Weidenfeld & Nicolson, 1988).

Glover, M., *Warfare in the Age of Bonaparte* (London, Cassell, 1980)

Griffith, P., *Art of War of Revolutionary France, 1789–1802* (London, Greenhill Books, 1999).

Haythornthwaite, P., *Napoleon's Campaigns in Italy* (London, Osprey, 1993).

–*Uniforms of the French Revolutionary Wars* (London, Arms and Armour, repr. 1999).

–*Weapons and Equipment of the Napoleonic Wars* (London, Arms and Armour 1998).

Hollins, D., *Marengo 1800* (Oxford, Osprey, 2000).

Howard, Michael, *War in European History* (Oxford, Oxford University Press, 1984).

Marcus, G.J., *The Age of Nelson* (New York, Viking Press, 1971).

Nosworthy, B., *Battle Tactics of Napoleon and his Enemies* (London, Constable, 1995).

Phipps, R.W., *The Armies of the First French Republic* (London, Oxford University Press, repr. 1999).

Rodger, A.B., *The War of the Second Coalition* (Oxford, Clarendon Press, 1964).

Rothenburg, G., *Napoleon's Great Adversary: Archduke Charles and the Austrian Army* (Bloomington, Indiana University Press, repr. 1995).

–*The Art of Warfare in the Age of Napoleon* (Bloomington, Indiana University Press, 1978).

Index